Bob Miller's

TALES FROM THE
LOS ANGELES
KINGS

Bob Miller
with Randy Schultz

SportsPublishingLLC.com

ISBN-10: 1-58261-811-9
ISBN-13: 978-1-58261-811-1

Publishers: Peter L. Bannon and Joseph J. Bannon Sr.
Senior managing editor: Susan M. Moyer
Acquisitions editor: Joseph J. Bannon Sr.
Developmental editor: Travis W. Moran
Art director: K. Jeffrey Higgerson
Dust jacket design: Joseph Brumleve
Interior layout: Heidi Norsen
Photo editor: Erin Linden-Levy

Sports Publishing L.L.C.
804 North Neil Street
Champaign, IL 61820
Phone: 1-877-424-2665
Fax: 217-363-2073
SportsPublishingLLC.com

Printed in the United States of America

CIP data available upon request.

To my wife, Judy, my daughter, Kristin, and my son, Kevin, for their support and love even though this job took me away from home on many nights.

To my late mother, Jo, who worked two jobs after my father's death so I would have the opportunity to pursue a college education and, ultimately, my dream.

–BM

This book is dedicated to the following:
Janet, my wife, who I love very much and I'm thankful for always being there with me. Damian, my grandson, who has once again allowed me to see life through a child's eyes.
Karla and Scott, my daughter and son-in-law, who have given me continued faith in the next generation.
Martha, my mom, who has been an inspiration to all for her fighting spirit as she battles cancer.
Carl and Betty, my father-in-law and mother-in-law.
Thanks for all of your constant love and support.
To all of the above, I love each and every one of you.
Thank You.

–RS

CONTENTS

ACKNOWLEDGMENTS vii

PREFACE ix

Chapter 1
PRESEASON—ON THE PATH TO ROYALTY 1

PREGAME 9

Chapter 2
FIRST PERIOD—THE OWNERS 13

FIRST INTERMISSION 33

Chapter 3
**SECOND PERIOD—JESTER'S TALES
IN THE KINGS' COURT** 39

SECOND INTERMISSION 73

Chapter 4
THIRD PERIOD—THE KINGDOM 79

FINAL INTERMISSION 123

Chapter 5
OVERTIME 129

Chapter 6
PLAYOFFS 139

AFTERWORD 173

ACKNOWLEDGMENTS

Thanks ...

To all the Kings owners, general managers, coaches, and players for their cooperation.

To all my on-air partners—Jim Minnick, Dan Avey, Rich Marotta, Pete Weber, Nick Nickson, and Jim Fox—for their friendship and help. It's been a pleasure working with you.

Thanks to the television producers—John Polich, Susan Stratton, Mark Stulberger, and Bob Borgen.

To all of you who helped me recall many of these stories and incidents, thank you.

To my friend, Phil Mendel, for his help and guidance. His enthusiasm for the game was infectious!

Thanks to John Wolf, Kings assistant to the general manager.

Thanks to Randy Schultz for his dedication in making this book a reality.

Thanks to Elisa Laird and Travis Moran of Sports Publishing for their editing skills.

Finally, thanks to all the Kings fans for your friendship and your critical comments—both good and bad.

–BM

PREFACE

In 1973, I started a wonderful journey in the National Hockey League with the Los Angeles Kings. Since that time, I have accumulated numerous stories about owners, general managers, coaches, players, broadcast partners, and humorous and strange incidents. Many of the stories I remembered from memory, others came from notes, and finally, I wanted to put them in writing to share with you.

While growing up in Chicago, I dreamed of being a Major League Baseball player or a sports announcer. Many days and nights, I would listen to various announcers: Bob Elson on the White Sox; Jack Brickhouse on the Sox, the Cubs, and the Bears; and Lloyd Pettit on the Blackhawks. Being in the Midwest, one was privileged to be able to listen to games from neighboring states, and I would always envy the play-by-play announcer who was at the game.

After playing two years of baseball at the University of Iowa—actually more sitting than playing—I realized that I'd better find another way of making a living. Iowa had an excellent campus radio station, WSUI, and students were given the opportunity to go on the air and make mistakes without being fired. It was a chance to improve my broadcasting skills.

In my junior and senior years at Iowa, I was able to do play-by-play of Hawkeye football and basketball. I was also fortunate in those years to be able to pick up some money and experience by broadcasting high school football and basketball each weekend on WQUA radio in Moline, Illinois.

While working for WQUA, I realized that play-by-play was more difficult than it sounded. In fact, I was fired after my first two football broadcasts. I thought I was ready and well prepared for those shows, but quickly found that I was in over my head. After the second game, the station's owner, G. LaVerne Flambo, told me he was going to make a change; and I knew he was making the

Bob Miller at a ceremony commemorating his 25th year with the Los Angeles Kings. *PHOTO PROVIDED COURTESY OF THE LOS ANGELES KINGS*

right decision. I wasn't ready. However, he didn't dismiss me completely—he asked me to come back in the winter and do basketball. The following season, I did both football and basketball. I will always be thankful to Mr. Flambo for giving me a second chance.

Being the broadcaster for the Kings has involved moments of extreme highs and extreme lows. I would rather have it that way, however, than to broadcast games in which I don't care who wins. I realize how fortunate I've been to be the "Voice of the Kings" for so many years and to be associated with so many outstanding people. To this date, I've broadcast over 2,600 games while weathering five owners, seven general managers, 14 coaches, six broadcast partners, and over 400 players.

I also know how fortunate I've been to have a family who picked up roots in Wisconsin and headed to California to follow *my* dream.

Thanks to all of you who have made that dream come true.

Bob Miller

PRESEASON

ON THE PATH TO ROYALTY

LOMBARDI

I believe the most important word in broadcasting—and probably in any job—is *preparation*. I didn't realize it at the time, but my first lesson in preparation came from the legendary coach of the Green Bay Packers Vince Lombardi.

In the early-1960s, while working at WITI-TV in Milwaukee, I had my first exposure to coach Lombardi. The station decided to do a half-hour feature entitled *A Week With The Packers*. The program would detail what the coaches and players do each day of the week leading up to Sunday's game.

Our aim was to interview Lombardi and then cut the questions out so that it would sound as if Lombardi was narrating the feature. For instance, if I asked "Coach, tell us what you do on Monday?" we wanted him to answer with, "On Monday, we have coaches meetings and prepare the game plan for the next game." This way the narration on the feature would be in Lombardi's own words.

I typed a three-page list of questions for the interview. When I arrived in Lombardi's office at Lambeau Field, I explained to him what we wished to accomplish. He said, "Let me see your questions." I handed him my list, and he silently looked them over. With a pen in hand, he proceeded to cross out questions he did not want to answer. Then he said, "Let's go."

The interview lasted about an hour, and when we finished, I thanked him and the crew and I went to lunch. Keep in mind those were the days before portable videotape cameras, so we shot everything on 16-millimeter film. While we were having lunch, the cameraman took the film to be developed. A short time later, he gave us some devastating news. There was a light leak in the camera, and the entire film was blank. The interview was lost. This was my worst nightmare. Vince Lombardi was a perfectionist; he did not tolerate mistakes from his players or anyone else. There were legendary stories about his temperamental explosions toward those who bungle an assignment. I knew I would have to go back to him, explain what happened, and wait for him to explode and kick me out of his office.

With all the bravery I could muster, I went back to his office, told him what had occurred, and watched as he stared at me, but he said nothing. Finally, he said, "Is your cameraman still here." I said he was, and Lombardi said, "Fine, get him in here and let's do it again."

I never realized it at the time, but this was my first lesson in preparation. I truly believe if he hadn't seen that I had spent a lot of time forming the questions, and typing them on paper, he never would have consented to a retake of the interview.

After we left his office, we still had some filming to do to complete the project. The final scene would be the Packers locker room, with all the equipment in the lockers, set up for Sunday's arrival of the players. Vince Lombardi's son, Vince Jr., worked for the Packers at that time while he attended college. I told him we needed someone to set up the lockers, and he responded, "Why not have Dad do it?"

I couldn't believe my ears: "Have his dad do it?"

Luckily, and probably for the sake of my life, I suddenly remembered the Packers equipment manager was nicknamed "Dad" Braisher. Can you imagine what would have happened if, after everything that went on in Lombardi's office, I waltzed back in and said to Vince, "Would you mind putting some shoulder pads and helmets in the lockers?"

You would not be reading this story today.

BART STARR

Those were exciting years to be covering the Packers. Under Lombardi, they won championships and claimed the first two Super Bowls. My one claim to fame, this many years later, is that I was at the so-called "Ice Bowl" game between the Packers and the Dallas Cowboys on December 31, 1967. This was for the National Football League championship, and in those days, television stations did not trade tape of game highlights as they do today. If your television station did not carry the live feed of the game, then you had to take a film crew and shoot film of the game to get highlights.

I was working at that time for WKOW-TV in Madison, Wisconsin, about a two-and-a-half-hour drive from Green Bay. When my clock radio went on that morning at 7:30, the first words I heard were, "It's 7:30 a.m. in Madison, and the temperature is 26 degrees below zero."

My wife, Judy, said, "You're not going to any football game in this weather."

I said, "I have to go, or we'll have no film of the game."

When the cameraman and I arrived at Lambeau Field, we were assigned with other television stations to the roof of the press box. There had been such a heavy request for coverage of the game that no room remained inside. To help shield us from the elements, which at this time had risen "all the way up" to 16 below zero, a canvas tarp had been stretched around the roof in an attempt to give us some relief from the wind and cold. It was of little help. We had to use heat lamps on the cameras, or they would freeze up and run at the wrong speed. The film was so brittle it would simply break apart in your hands as you attempted to thread the camera.

The game was a classic with the Packers making a last-ditch drive down the field, scoring the winning touchdown when quarterback Bart Starr sneaked into the end zone behind the block of Jerry Kramer. As we ran to the locker room for postgame interviews, I literally had no feeling in my legs from the knees down. I'll never forget the sight of Packers linebacker Ray Nitschke in the locker room with his jersey off and his upper body covered with cuts that looked as if someone had slashed him with razor blades. These marks were from falling on the jagged edges of the frozen field.

I must also say that, in all of my 46 years of professional broadcasting, only one athlete has ever sent me a letter when the season concluded. That letter read:

> Dear Bob,
>
> We want to take this opportunity to thank you again for the genuine interest, support and consideration you have shown the Packers during the past season. We are very happy to be associated with folks such as you and just wanted to tell you again that we appreciate all that you do for us.
> Best Wishes.
>
> Sincerely,
> Bart Starr

VAN PATRICK

Many times, you have someone you admire but have never met in person; and then the meeting doesn't turn out quite as you imagined.

As a youngster in Chicago, I always watched the annual Thanksgiving Day National Football League game between the Green Bay Packers and the Detroit Lions. The announcer was Van Patrick, who had a classic voice that I always associated with that particular game.

Years later, as I was covering the Packers, I was in the press box at Milwaukee County Stadium, and I met Van Patrick face to face. I introduced myself and told him how much I enjoyed his announcing of that Thanksgiving Day game. He said "Thank you," and with that he reached for the fly of his pants and said, "Do you have a safety pin? The zipper on my fly is broken."

JESSE OWENS

In this business, I've been fortunate to meet and interview many famous and interesting people. None, however, made the lasting impression on me like the late Olympic track star, Jesse Owens.

In the early 1960s, while working at WITI-TV in Milwaukee I covered the Milwaukee Journal Indoor Track meet at the Milwaukee Arena. As the cameraman and I entered the building, I spotted Owens. I asked him if we could do a short interview, and he graciously consented. That "short" interview turned out to be about 30 minutes long because his answers and comments were so thoughtful and intriguing.

I asked why his records, which stood for so many years, finally had begun to be broken. I expected the standard answer that records are made to be broken, but his answer amazed me.

"Because of the prenatal care available today," he said. "Babies come into this world in better physical shape than ever before and have advantages that, in my day, we never had."

I asked him about Hitler refusing to shake his hand at the 1936 Olympics in Germany and he said, "I had a wonderful time at the Olympics, and I'm having a wonderful time at this track meet tonight. Where Hitler is right now is of no concern to me."

Jesse Owens was the most gracious and most interesting person I have ever interviewed.

BASLER

When I was broadcasting University of Wisconsin hockey from 1968 to 1973, there were times we used a charter-air service called Basler Airlines out of Oshkosh, Wisconsin. The owner was Warren Basler, and his wife was the flight attendant on some trips. The equipment used was a DC-3, a twin-engine propeller plane.

On one trip from Madison, Wisconsin, to Ann Arbor, Michigan, we left Madison in a raging snowstorm. It was so bad you literally couldn't see the tip of the wing. The players pleaded with Coach Bob Johnson to fly the next day when the storm was over, but Johnson said we had to fly that day. As we taxied out to take off, our goaltender, John Anderson, was reciting the Lord's Prayer with a blanket over his head.

At this point, Mrs. Basler, stood at the front of the plane, and, with her hands cupped around her mouth, she shouted, "Gentlemen, welcome aboard Basler Airlines." I was horrified that the plane had no intercom as she continued, "Our captain today is Warren Basler, and I am Mrs. Basler."

We made it to Michigan, and after the Saturday night game, we headed for a deserted Ann Arbor airport. Most of the flights used the Detroit metro airport so the Ann Arbor airport didn't even have a control tower. As we approached the plane, we heard a thumping noise and discovered it was Captain Basler knocking snow off of the wing with a broom. He wouldn't start the engines until we were all aboard, and it was a bitterly cold night with no heat in the cabin. As we taxied for take-off, I turned on the little reading light above my head, and Mrs. Basler raced down the aisle and said to me, "Turn off that light. We need all the power we can get for take-off."

I couldn't believe that little light was going to determine whether we achieved flight.

We flew over Lake Michigan for a couple of hours, and Captain Basler then informed us that we would land in Milwaukee to refuel. Milwaukee is the first city on the West side of the Lake, and I thought, "We have just flown over Lake Michigan on any icy night; and at the first site of land, we have to refuel?" Madison was only 70 miles farther, and we didn't have enough fuel to make it.

When we landed in Milwaukee, Captain Basler was walking through the cabin when one of the players asked what happened to a plane that took off ahead of us from Michigan. Basler said, "Oh, he turned and went back. There weren't many who would have done what we did tonight."

With that, several players declared they would not fly the rest of the way to Madison and instead would take a bus.

PREGAME

GETTING THE JOB

I actually thought I had the Kings radio-TV job in 1972 when I was working in Madison, Wisconsin, doing radio broadcasts of University of Wisconsin hockey. An acquaintance of mine had moved to Southern California and told me the Kings announcer, Jiggs McDonald, was moving to Atlanta to become the announcer for the expansion Flames. I sent a résumé and tape to Lakers announcer Chick Hearn, who had been given the job of finding a replacement by Kings owner Jack Kent Cooke. Chick called me and said he liked my material and was going to recommend me for the job. That was in April 1972.

Several weeks went by, and I heard nothing from the Kings. While on a weekend vacation in Northern Wisconsin, I picked up the Sunday *Milwaukee Journal* and saw a short item about Hearn's son being found dead from a drug overdose in North Hollywood.

Obviously Chick had more on his mind than my job offer.

That June, I still had heard nothing from the Kings, but when I attended a National Sports Information Directors Conference in Chicago, I ran into Don Anderson, the sports information director at the University of Southern California, who told me the Kings had hired a local announcer, Roy Storey.

A few weeks later I called Chick and pretended not to have heard about the hiring of Storey.

"Has a decision been made yet on the Kings job?" I asked.

"Didn't anyone call you?"

He told me that after his son's death he left town, but before he left he told the Kings to hire me.

I later found out that Cooke always had to let you know he was in charge. If you came to him with three persons to hire and you picked one, he would pick another just to show you he was the boss. That was what happened to Chick.

I stayed at Wisconsin, which was fortunate because the Badgers won the NCAA hockey championship that season. That has been the only championship team I've been connected with thus far. It was great.

During the season I had heard that the Kings were ready to make another announcer change. I sent Hearn some updated tapes and again let him know of my interest. That April, I was in Chicago and found out the L.A. Lakers were coming to town to play the Bulls. I found out which hotel they were staying at and waited three hours in the lobby to meet Hearn in person.

Chick was always in a rush and our meeting lasted about two minutes.

"I may have something for you in a couple of months," he said as we parted.

On June 5, 1973, Chick called me and asked if my wife and I could come to California to talk about the job.

We landed in L.A. the next day, and it was 106 degrees. Chick and Kings general manager Larry Regan met us and took us to lunch in Marina Del Rey. We sat on the restaurant patio overlooking the marina with hundreds of yachts and sailboats; I took in the beautiful view.

"How much will I have to pay them to get this job?" I wondered.

A few weeks later Chick called me again and told me to come out and sign my contract.

When I arrived in July, the Kings told me they had rented a car for me, a small Plymouth Omega for $14.95 per day. I was to drive to Mr. Cooke's mansion in Bel Air and meet Larry Regan there.

"Whatever you do, don't tell Cooke that we rented that car," Regan instructed. "If he asks, tell him it's your car."

This was my first indication I wasn't going to get rich working for Cooke; after all, the car was only $14.95 a day.

When I arrived at Mr. Cooke's house, I identified myself and two iron gates swung open revealing a courtyard, which was where I parked. During the meeting Cooke spoke with Regan about me as if I wasn't there.

"Larry, how much are we paying this young man?" he asked.

Regan replied, "$22,000, Mr. Cooke."

"God, Larry!" he hollered. "I told you $20,000."

Here was Cooke, a multimillionaire, trying to take $2,000 dollars from me. As it turned out, I got the $22,000 and it was double what I was making in Wisconsin.

"For God's sake," he commanded, "don't tell anyone how much you're making."

"Don't worry, Mr. Cooke, I'm as embarrassed about it as you are."

Cooke's home office looked out on the courtyard, and during our conversation he looked out the window.

"Whose little car is that?" he asked.

"It's mine, Mr. Cooke," I replied.

"I like little cars. I have two of them myself, a Mercedes and a Maserati."

I was to sign my contract a couple of days later, and when I called home, my wife told me the Pittsburgh Penguins had called.

"What did they want?" I asked.

"They want to know if you want to broadcast their games," she answered.

I couldn't believe it. After all those years of rejection, now two teams wanted me to sign.

I was reluctant to tell Chick about the other offer because I was ready to sign with the Kings, and I knew Chick wanted this off his mind. I decided to tell Chick about this development.

"Bob, you've got to give the Penguins a call and listen to their offer," he said calmly to my surprise. "Don't ever ignore someone's offer of a job. If it's better than the Kings' offer, take it, but if it's similar, I think you'll be happier here."

I called Pittsburgh and the offer was not nearly as good as the Kings.

I signed my contract for $22,000 and basked in the Los Angeles sun.

2

FIRST PERIOD

THE OWNERS

JACK KENT COOKE

Jack Kent Cooke, the former owner of the Los Angeles Kings, Lakers, and the Forum was small in physical stature but was a giant in the sports and business world. By the time he passed away on April 6, 1997 at age 84, he had accumulated close to a billion dollars. He didn't inherit this money; he started out selling soap to hotels, and then selling encyclopedia sets door to door in his native Canada.

The story goes that one Sunday evening, Cooke and his new wife found themselves in a little town in Saskatchewan with no money to buy dinner that night. Cooke found the home of a high school principal and convinced him to give him a five-dollar deposit on a set of encyclopedias. He then had enough money for food.

He stood only about 5-foot-9, was always impeccably dressed, in a dark suit or blazer always with a silk handerkerchief in the breast pocket. He had a booming stentorian voice. He peered at you through slits in his eyelids, but he could look right through you—especially if he was upset over something you had said or done.

One could use any number of adjectives to describe his personality: tyrannical, overbearing, shrewd, impressive, intelligent, and dynamic. He was the epitome of a "hands-on" owner, one who was domineering and controlled every facet of his empire, which included not only the Kings, Lakers, and Forum, but also in later years the Chrysler Building in New York City, TelePrompter, and the Washington Redskins of the National Football League. He possessed a wonderful command of the English language and never let anyone forget it, and at times he could be quite condescending. At one time he owned one of the largest radio stations in Toronto, CKEY. In those days, due to the "blue laws" no stores were open on Sundays. Cooke had one man who had worked for some 20 years at the radio station. One day this employee asked Mr. Cooke if he could have Sundays off, feeling that after 20 years he deserved weekends to himself. Mr. Cooke replied, "What would you do in Toronto with Sundays off? Even I wouldn't know what to do if I didn't have my yacht."

I always admired the fact that he was a self-made multimillionaire, had an estimated $900 million when he passed away, but he left a lot to be desired in the manner in which he treated employees. Because of that attitude he lost a lot of good and talented people who simply said they had had enough and quit their jobs.

Employees lived and worked in fear of raising Mr. Cooke's ire. So much so that we always had a lookout who each morning would watch for Mr. Cooke's Bentley to pull into the Forum parking lot. The sentry would then, in Paul Revere fashion, come down the hallway informing us "Mr. Cooke is coming, Mr. Cooke is coming."

Upon hearing that announcement secretaries would pretend to be on the phone, and office doors would quickly shut so that no one would have to see or talk to him. If Cooke saw you, he would usually greet you in a friendly manner, "Good morning, Bob," but then by the time he arrived in his office he would think of something he was upset with you about and summon you to his office. The summons would come in the form of an announcement on the Forum public address system and would boom throughout the building, "BOB MILLER, REPORT TO MR. COOKE'S OFFICE." Everyone then knew you were in trouble and would actually mock you and laugh at you as you headed for Cooke's office, much like a grade school pupil summoned to the principal's office for a scolding.

THE ANNOUNCEMENT

Late afternoon on Friday, June 13, 1975, those of us in the Kings' hockey office were told to report to the office of owner Jack Kent Cooke—general manager Jake Milford, public relations director Mike Hope, my broadcast partner, Dan Avey, and me. When we arrived, we were surprised to see members of the L.A. Lakers staff already seated. Included were Lakers GM Pete Newell, coach Bill Sharman, announcer Chick Hearn, and Forum publicity director Dick White. I was curious to know why, if this was a hockey announcement, were all the basketball folks there; and if it pertained to basketball, why were we there?

At this time, reports arose that the Kings were close to signing Detroit Red Wing star Marcel Dionne, and I hoped that was the reason for the meeting.

Cooke, seated at his desk, announced in his booming voice: "I have called all of you here to announce to you that today we have signed ... the greatest basketball player in the world, Kareem Abdul-Jabbar. I was sitting on a sofa to Cooke's right, and I guess my face showed my disappointment at not hearing Dionne's name.

Cooke looked at me and hollered, "What's wrong with you, Bob? Don't you know anything about sports? I just made this tremendous announcement, and you're sitting there like a bump on a log. Chick, did you see his reaction?"

"Yes, Jack," Chick said, "I did." (Chick was the only employee I knew who could call Cooke "Jack" and get away with it.) At this point, I wasn't too happy with Chick.

"Mr. Cooke," I replied, "I thought you were going to say you had signed Marcel Dionne for the Kings."

"That will be for another day," Cooke replied. "We are going to have a press conference Monday morning here at the Forum, and it will be the greatest sports press conference in history. If any of this leaks out before Monday, you are all fired."

I thought, "This is great … we are going to try to sneak into town—without anyone noticing—a seven-foot tall athlete who played basketball for UCLA? It can't be done. "

"The press conference will be held at 10 a.m." Cooke continued. "When should we notify the media?"

He called upon Dick White, who answered, "We should call the media at 9 a.m. Monday morning."

"Nine a.m. Monday morning?" Cooke bewilderedly asked. "Bob, what do you think?"

I knew he wasn't too pleased with Dick White's answer, so I said, "I think Monday morning is too short notice. I think the hockey people should come in here late Sunday night, and when the sports shows are finished, we call the television and radio stations and inform them of the press conference. That way, they will still think it's hockey related and not basketball."

"Right you are," said Cooke. "Dick White, what am I paying you for?"

I may not have been too pleased with Chick, but Dick White was definitely displeased with me. The meeting was becoming very bizarre.

Again, Cooke turned to me and said, "Bob ..." and at that point, I was just hoping that he'd leave me alone and ask someone else. "Bob, you are from *Sports Illustrated*, and you're assigned to cover this press conference. When it's over, do you want a sit-down luncheon or a buffet with chicken cacciatore?"

By then, I was getting into the routine. "Mr. Cooke," I said, "I would be so excited about this announcement and so anxious to write my story that I would like a buffet with chicken cacciatore."

"Right again!" Cooke exclaimed.

At that point, I was thinking, "Can I leave now? I've answered two questions right, and it's not going to get any better than this." On that Sunday night, some of us from the Kings office came in and made calls to the television and radio-station sports departments. Some rumors had arisen about this deal on the air. Cooke came in that Monday morning about nine o'clock, and I'd never seen him so excited. He was dressed to the "nines" and could hardly wait to make his monumental announcement.

The Forum floor was empty aside from a stage at the south end, where the home teams enter and exit the floor. On this stage, Cooke had the operations department put two hockey nets and two basketball backboards to further the charade of whether this was a hockey or basketball announcement. Shortly after he arrived, Cooke came to my office and said, "Bob, let's rehearse the news conference."

He gathered several employees, such as Chick Hearn, who would make the announcement; the organist, who was instructed to play the Lakers March at the proper time; and the spotlight operator, who would beam the light on black curtains through which Abdul-Jabbar would enter.

Hearn went to the podium, made a phony announcement to maintain secrecy, and then Cooke cued the organist. Satisfied, he returned to his office. About 15 minutes later, he came back again. "Bob, let's rehearse once more." Again, Hearn went to the podium, the organist climbed to his perch, the spotlight operator was summoned, and we rehearsed—it went off without a hitch.

At 10 a.m., the Forum floor was filled with numerous reporters, television cameras, and microphones. At a table next to the stage and near the podium sat Jack Kent Cooke, Pete Newell, and Bill Sharman. Chick Hearn approached the podium, and, in a voice that sounded as if he were hyperventilating, he made this announcement:

"Ladies and gentlemen, introducing the newest Los Angeles Laker, the most dominant player in the NBA—Kareem Abdul-Jabbar."

With that, the lights dimmed; the organist played; and the spotlight focused on the curtains. No one came out. The music continued and, still, no one appeared.

By this time, some of the reporters began to laugh along with other members of the audience, and I thought, "This is so embarrassing for Cooke that we'll all be fired."

Finally, a pair of black hands parted the curtain, which relieved all of us, feeling, "Abdul-Jabbar must be here." Unfortunately, a uniformed security guard stuck his hat and head through the opening. Now, the laughter increased. A short time later, Kareem appeared, looking confused as he peered into the darkened arena. The reason he was late? The Lakers had hidden him in the locker room, and he went to use the bathroom, where he couldn't hear the announcement.

As it turned out, Cooke was still elated, and no one was fired.

SCOOTING LIKE A DATSUN

One morning in the fall of 1975, Mr. Cooke called my broadcast partner, Dan Avey, and me into his office and told us he wanted to run 14 30-second commercials per period in our Kings broadcasts. At that time, the National Hockey League would not stop the game for radio or TV commercial timeouts. I told Mr. Cooke that I didn't think it would be possible to air that many commercials, because at the time we were running only four per period, and some nights, due to the pace of the game, it was almost impossible to get those on the air.

Our main sponsor at the time was Datsun (now Nissan). "Then you will mention the sponsor's name in a different way," Cooke explained. "For instance you will say, 'There's Marcel Dionne scooting down the ice like a Datsun.' What do you think of that?"

As I listened to him, I remembered the other meetings I had had in Cooke's office with Lakers announcer Chick Hearn. Cooke would come up with some hare-brained ideas, and Chick would respond, "That's a wonderful idea."

As Chick replied, I'd think, "Chick, what are you agreeing to? That's one of the worst ideas I've ever heard."

Then when the meeting was over and we'd walk down the hallway, Chick would complain to me, "That silly bastard. We aren't going to do any of that stuff."

Well, I was determined to stop this idea in its tracks.

"Mr. Cooke," I stated matter-of-factly, "I can't imagine saying that once let alone 80 times a year."

Cooke exploded.

"I'm sick and tired of your attitude!" he thundered. "Do you know how many people want your job, and they're this close [holding his thumb and forefinger a half-inch apart] to getting it."

I smiled at him without saying a word in response, and that set him off even more.

"WIPE THAT SILLY GRIN OFF YOUR FACE AND GET OUT OF MY SIGHT!"

I stood up to leave.

"SIT DOWN!" he roared before I could even take a step toward the door.

Jack Kent Cooke—Kings Owner, 1967-1979. PHOTO BY WEN ROBERTS PHOTOGRAPHY INK

I sat.

"Right now it's 11:30 a.m.," he continued. "I want both of you back in here at 2 p.m., and you'd better have some answers for me. NOW, GET OUT!"

Dan and I left his office and walked down the hall. As we did, several secretaries who worked about 100 feet from Cooke's office approached us.

"What did you two guys do?" they asked.

They had heard Cooke yelling at us from that far away.

"Are we fired?" Dan asked with concern.

"Not until 2 p.m.," I replied. "Let's go have some lunch and talk about this."

Over lunch at the Forum Club the conversation turned away from the seriousness of the ultimatum to jokes about the situation.

"You could say, 'The Kings have scored 10 seconds after the start of the game,'" Dan suggested coyly, "and I could say, 'Dat-soon, Dat-soon.'"

That sparked another idea.

"We could give Marcel Dionne No. 280Z," I chuckled, "and Butch Goring could be B-210." (The 280Z and B210 were Datsun model numbers.)

Finally, at 2 p.m. we reappeared in Cooke's office. He stared at me through those beady eyes.

"Well?" he said, commanding an answer.

"Mr. Cooke, we could say, 'The score on the Datsun scoreboard is Kings 2, Montreal 1,' or 'This is the Datsun-Kings radio network.'"

There was silence as he looked at me.

"My, my," he stated with condescension in his voice, "aren't you a brilliant fellow?

"Now both of you get out of here."

That was the last we heard about Dionne scooting down the ice like a Datsun.

MR. COOKE CALLING

On December 2, 1976, Rich Marotta and I were doing a simulcast as the Kings played the Montreal Canadiens at the Forum in Montreal. In those days, we didn't have a television studio in the arena, so between periods, Rich would go down to ice level and interview a player. This particular night, the first period ended with the score 1-0, and I was on camera ready to throw to Rich, who was at rinkside. The problem was, Rich's microphone wouldn't work, so I got the signal to keep filling until they could fix the problem. I kept talking and talking, and still they gave me the signal to stretch. With the score 1-0, there wasn't much to talk about, but I kept going; and in my mind, I was thinking, "I'm doing a pretty good job of filling this time." Finally, I got the signal to throw it to Rich.

Just then, the phone rang in our broadcast booth, and the engineer said to me, "It's for you."

"Who's calling me here in Montreal while we're on the air?" I asked.

"Someone from Los Angeles," he replied.

I picked up the phone, and it was someone from the L.A. Forum. He informed me that Mr. Cooke had just called. I figured Cooke had called to congratulate me on the masterful job I'd just done to fill time while we were waiting on Rich's microphone.

"What did he want?" I asked.

"He said for you to quit hogging the mic and let Rich talk once in a while."

***

Cooke had a habit of calling employees during Kings games from his owner's box at the L.A. Forum. One night, he called engineer Scotty Collins in the engine room.

"Scotty, what's the temperature in this building?" Cooke asked.

"It's 68 degrees, Mr. Cooke," Scotty answered.

"I want it [at] 67," Cooke replied.

"Yes, Sir, Mr. Cooke." Scotty told me he had been sitting with his feet on the desk listening to the game, and he never moved from that position. A short time later, Cooke called again.

"Scotty, what's the temperature in this building?"

"Sixty-seven degrees, Mr. Cooke," Scotty told him.

"I thought so," Cooke said. "It feels much better in here."

***

I would get calls from Cooke right during the play-by-play. Cooke's private box was at the north end of the arena; and before we televised home games, he would sit in his box with a radio to his ears and a pair of binoculars aimed at our broadcast location. That was quite intimidating. Cooke felt that each Kings broadcast was a three-hour commercial for his building, The Fabulous Forum, and the events that would take place there—he especially wanted us to promote season-seat sales.

A scientific experiment you may have heard about involved a professor of physiology named Ivan Pavlov and his dog. To elicit a conditioned response, Pavlov would ring a bell and then feed his dog. Eventually, when his dog heard the bell, it would salivate, knowing that he was going to be fed. I told people I was like Pavlov's dog. Every time I heard a phone ring in the press box during a broadcast, I would immediately say, on the air, "Don't forget, Kings fans, season seats are still available," and I would give a phone number. It didn't matter whether the phone call was for someone five rows behind me—I was conditioned.

***

One day before a game, Mr. Cooke said to me, "I'm going to have several friends at the game tonight. They are not familiar with the game. We'll be listening to your broadcast, and I want you to make sure you identify every single line change and every player in that game."

During the first period, I felt I was doing an excellent job of what Cooke required, although I did miss one Philadelphia line change. The buzzer sounded ending the period, and the phone next to me rang immediately.

When I answered, Cooke thundered, "YOU'RE NOT DOING WHAT I TOLD YOU TO DO! NOW YOU'D BETTER START DOING A BETTER JOB NEXT PERIOD!"

***

Early in my career with the Kings, I was aware a double standard existed between Kings play-by-play and Lakers play-by-play. Chick Hearn was the longtime and brilliant announcer for the Lakers, and I would listen to his broadcasts to learn something from the Hall of Famer. I noticed how Chick, at times, would be relentless in his criticism of the Lakers, saying things like, "Happy Hairston blows the layup. ... He leads the world in blown layups."

So, I thought that was the way to do the broadcast.

On our next broadcast, the Kings had a 2-on-1 break, and the player with the puck didn't shoot; nor did his pass connect with a teammate. I said, on the air, "He had a chance to score and passed the puck. Why did he pass? He should have shot."

The next day, I made the trip to Cooke's office, and he said, "I don't ever want to hear you second-guess what a player is doing. It's much easier for you to see the play from where you're sitting than it is on the ice."

***

One night, during a broadcast, I said something funny or made a joke of something on the air, and the next morning, I was called—once again—into Mr. Cooke's office.

"Dear boy," he said to me, "do you know who my next-door neighbor is?"

"No, Mr. Cooke," I answered. "I have no idea."

"Well," he said, "it's Jerry Lewis. He has 14 joke writers; you don't have any. Don't try to be funny."

CONTRACT WHILE WET

The end of my first five-year contract with the Kings was at the end of the 1977-78 season. The Kings that year had finished third in the Norris Division and were getting ready to play the Toronto Maple Leafs in the first round of the playoffs.

On a Sunday afternoon in April my wife and I were swimming and relaxing around the pool at our home, when the phone rang. My wife answered and said to me, "It's for you, it's Mr. Cooke." I said, "Get out of here, he wouldn't be calling me at home."

I got to the phone dripping wet, and Cooke, who never identified himself, he just figured you'd know who it was said, "Bob, I want to talk about your new contract." This took me by surprise, and I was no match for Cooke as far as finance was concerned and especially not while dripping wet on my patio.

He said, "I want you to sign for another five years. Get a paper and pencil and write down these figures. The first year $28,000; the second year, $32,000; the third year, $35,000; the fourth year, 39,000 and the fifth year $43,000, what do you think of that?"

I wanted to make more money but I was scared to mention that to Cooke fearing he would be really upset, but I plunged ahead and said, "Mr. Cooke, I would like to make more money than that." There was a pause and then he said, "Here are the new numbers, write them down." And again he went through the first year, the second year, the third year etc., all with new numbers.

I then felt that I needed more money in years four and five, but I was terrified to make that proposal. However, with all the bravery I could muster I said, "Mr. Cooke, I would like to see the figures for years four and five increased." Holding my breath, my eyes squeezed shut; I then waited for the explosion from the other end of the line. Again, after a pause, Cooke said, "Here are the new numbers, write them down. Year one $35,000; year two $40,000; year three $45,000; year four $51,000 … then he abruptly paused and said in his booming voice, "My God, we're getting into astronomical numbers."

I thought, "For someone who was signing players for a hell of a lot more, these numbers were not astronomical."

He wanted to know if I was satisfied with the final numbers, and I sensed they were indeed final. A few weeks before this I had received a call from Bob Pulford, then general manager and coach of the Chicago Blackhawks. Pully wanted to know my contract situation and told me not to sign again until I contacted him because he would like me to come to Chicago. When Cooke called I had not yet heard anything from Pulford, so I told thanked Cooke for his offer, but told him I was concentrating on the playoffs and couldn't give him an answer at this time. He asked when I would make a decision and I told him when the playoffs are over. He said, "Fine, and you call me personally with your decision, do not deal with anyone else in the organization."

As bad luck would have it, the Kings were eliminated in two games of a best two-of-three series. However, I thought, I told Cooke when the playoffs ended, that could mean the NHL playoffs not just the Kings playoffs. I kept calling Pulford to get an answer but he said he had not yet talked to Bill Wirtz, the Blackhawks owner. As the weeks went by I finally told Pulford I need an answer or Cooke would get upset and I'd be out of the Kings job. Finally Pulford told me Mr. Wirtz wanted to hire someone from Cincinnati. I said that's fine, called Cooke and accepted his offer for five more seasons.

THE MAGAZINE

In the mid-1980s before a game in Washington, D.C., a writer told me he was doing an article on Jack Kent Cooke for the *Los Angeles Magazine* and he heard that I had some Cooke stories. He interviewed me and printed the stories I related to him. About a week after the magazine came out, the author called me and asked, "Did you read the article?" When I said yes, he asked, "Did I quote you correctly?" I again said yes, and he said Cooke was very upset and told him, "Miller was a disgruntled employee and he's spreading lies." I told the writer that everything I told him was true, and he said, "That's good because I'm writing it again for *Washingtonian Magazine*." At that time Cooke lived in the D.C. area in Virginia.

A few weeks later, I got a call from my former broadcast partner, Dan Avey. He told me Cooke had called him while in Los Angeles and even though Dan had not spoken to Cooke for some 12 years, Cooke didn't say hello or how are you he just started, "Dan, what is Miller up to? He's spreading falsehoods."

Cooke at this time owned the *Los Angeles Daily News* so I decided to call him and talk with him about the articles. I phoned the newspaper and was told that he was leaving California that night, but he would call me back.

The Kings were opening the 1988-89 season that night and were playing games on Thursday, Saturday, and Sunday. By Sunday, I had not heard from Cooke. I had made a list of points

I was going to make during our phone call, and since I no longer worked for him, I was determined not to be intimidated.

After the weekend games I was home on Monday morning having almost forgotten about the call to Cooke when the phone rang and the woman said, "Mr. Miller, please hold for Mr. Cooke." I panicked. My notes were upstairs, and I was downstairs.

Cooke came on the phone and bellowed, "You called me!"

I said, "Yes, Mr. Cooke. I understand you're upset over the magazine articles."

He said, "I'm more than upset. I'm mortified, that you would spread such lies… Goodbye."

And he hung up.

A week later I told the story to Kings owner Bruce McNall who got a laugh out of it, and then I said, "Bruce, don't ever sell the team back to Cooke, or I'm the first one to go."

BUSS' BEDROOM

One of the most bizarre events in Kings history took place in the spring of 1984. Before the NHL amateur draft in June, the Kings public relations department decided it would be advantageous to invite the press to view videotape of young junior and collegiate hockey players who were eligible for the draft that year and who might be picked by the Kings. That year the Kings had Chicago's No.1 pick, which was the sixth pick overall.

The draft preview was held at "Pickfair," the Beverly Hills mansion of Kings owner Dr. Jerry Buss. It was named Pickfair because at one time it was the home of film stars Mary Pickford and Douglas Fairbanks.

As I approached the house that day, the front door was ajar and no one answered the bell. I entered into the foyer when one of the house staff appeared. I told him I was there for the Kings

Dr. Jerry Buss–Kings Owner, 1979-1988. PHOTO BY WEN ROBERTS PHOTOGRAPHY INK

meeting and he said, "It's upstairs in Dr. Buss' bedroom." I was surprised by this, but ventured upstairs and sure enough, folding chairs were placed around the bed and snacks and drinks were set out. Most of us in attendance looked at each other with raised eyebrows, thinking this was a peculiar place to hold this meeting.

Dr. Buss came in, dressed in jeans and a sport shirt and reclined on his bed as we watched videotape of hockey players on the TV at the foot of the bed.

The Kings' No. 1 pick that year was defenseman Craig Redmond, who had great potential but ended up playing only two full seasons and portions of two others with the Kings. He played 170 games with 13 goals, 58 assists, and 71 points and was traded to Edmonton in 1988.

McNALL AND THE MIGHTY DUCKS

During the 1992-93 season the NHL, with Kings owner Bruce McNall as chairman of the Board of Governors, convinced the Disney Company and its chairman, Michael Eisner, to put an expansion team in Anaheim, California. That was a mere 35 miles from the home of the Kings. The price for a new team to join the league was $50 million, and McNall would get half of that as compensation for allowing another team into his territory. In his book, *Fun While It Lasted*, McNall said he received $12.5 million in cash and a note at a low-interest rate for the remainder.

I have always felt that was one of McNall's worst decisions, but as he said in his book, "I needed the money." The Kings were drawing capacity crowds with Wayne Gretzky, and all this did was take some hockey fans away from the Kings and send them to Anaheim. This was the season the Kings went to the Stanley Cup Finals, and without a team in Anaheim the Kings probably would have had a waiting list for season tickets.

Bruce McNall—Kings Owner, 1988-1994. *PHOTO COURTESY OF THE LOS ANGELES KINGS*

My partner, Jim Fox, and I were doing a Kings telecast the day the new team in Anaheim was named. The Disney Company named them after a successful Disney movie, *The Mighty Ducks*. On the air I said to Jim, "Did you hear what they named the new team in Anaheim?" Jim said, "Yes, they'll be called the Mighty Ducks," and I said, "Yes, and as an expansion team they'll also be known as the Dead Ducks, the Lame Ducks, and the Sitting Ducks."

The next day I was out Christmas shopping, and when I returned home, my wife said, "Michael Eisner called and wants you to phone him." I thought she was kidding. I also thought he was either upset over what we had said on the air about his team or he was going to offer me a job. When I called him back, he said, "Bob, thanks for the mention last night. I was watching your telecast, and it was nice of you to talk about us."

I guess the saying is true, any publicity is good publicity.

LIMO RIDE

At times when the Kings were on the road, owner Bruce McNall would fly with the team, but instead of taking the team bus to the hotel, he would have a limousine meet him at the airport. One night after a flight to Chicago, Kings travel coordinator Ron Muniz told my partner Nick Nickson and me that McNall wanted us to ride with him in the limo. The Kings had lost that night and I thought McNall was angry about something we had said on the air. As we drove away from the airport, McNall said nothing.

"Bruce, to what do we owe this privilege of riding in the limo?" I asked, finally needing to know if he was upset.

I was waiting for him to explode when he said, "You two are the only ones who didn't screw up tonight, so I wanted to give you a limo ride."

FIRST INTERMISSION

THE SHMOOS

After the conclusion of the 1976-77 season my broadcast partner Rich Marotta asked me what we were supposed to do in the off-season.

"I'm not sure," I told him. "But don't go asking anyone or they will come up with a job for us."

I told Rich to stay home and out of sight. A few days later he called me and told me he wasn't comfortable staying home and that he felt he should be working.

I knew it was a question of time before he got us into trouble so I devised a little trouble for us. A few days later I found Rich at the Forum.

"Well now you've done it," I told him. "Mr. Cooke wants us to sell advertising on the shmoos."

"What is a shmoo?" he asked confused.

"They are the waist-high concrete pylons in the parking lot that direct the traffic," I explained with a smile.

"The term *shmoo* came from the *Lil Abner* comic strip in which characters called shmoos kept multiplying."

Rich couldn't believe what I was telling him, but I assured him it was true. We were going to have to peddle the team to every Mom and Pop shop.

"I swear. We have to go up and down Manchester Boulevard and tell merchants they can buy a half a shmoo for $15 or a whole shmoo for $25."

Later that morning I let Kings general manager Jake Milford in on my scheme and that I was having lunch with Rich and his dad at the Forum Club.

Jake, who could put anyone on with a straight face, smiled and said he would join us, so the four of us went out for "working" lunch.

"How is it going, Jake?" I asked, making small talk.

"That Mr. Cooke is driving me crazy. He's on my back about everything … and you two guys," he complained while pointing to Rich and myself, "when are you going to get started on selling those shmoos?"

"What in the hell is a shmoo?" Rich's dad asked.

Every time we mentioned selling the shmoos Rich's head dropped in despair. He was so depressed for having to do something so demeaning. Jake and I left in high spirits, knowing by the down look on Rich's face that we had hooked him.

After lunch Rich's dad called him.

"I was looking at those shmoos as I drove out of the parking lot," he said. "They're all cracked and chipped. If you ever came into my business and tried to sell me one of those things, I'd kick you right out on the street."

This put Rich into another spasm.

Later I called Rich to come to my office, and I pretended I had the president of Sizzler restaurants on the phone.

Rich Marotta—Kings Color Commentator, 1976-1979. *PHOTO COURTESY OF KFI RADIO*

"He wants to buy a shmoo," I assured Rich as I handed him a 12-inch ruler. "He wants to know how big they are, so do me a favor and go out to the parking lot and measure one."

He looked at me skeptically, but after I insisted, he trudged off to measure the shmoo. A group of us who were in on the joke hid in the entrance of the Forum to watch Rich. He went to a shmoo, held the ruler at the bottom of the concrete, marked where the top of the ruler ended with his hand, and then used his hand as a base for the next 12 inches. Once he was done, I raced back to my office before he got there.

"They are 36 inches high," he reported.

"Do you know how big around they are?" I asked.

"What? No!" he responded as his face reddened.

Later that night I told my wife the story.

"You should call Rich and tell him it's a joke," she said.

"I'll wait a few days. Let him stew over it a bit."

Well, he did stew over it. Unbeknownst to me, that night Rich called some broadcasting friends of his, Cleve Herman at KFWB and Allin Slate at KNX, and said he had a real crisis and had to talk with them. They picked him up, and on the way to Dodger Stadium for a ballgame they waited for Rich to drop this bombshell.

"Rich, what is this big crisis?" one of them asked.

After a pause Rich told them.

"I have to sell advertising on the shmoos."

"What is a shmoo?" they asked.

When Rich told them, they burst out laughing, which made Rich feel worse. After that Rich met with his dad and Uncle Pete to discuss his dilemma. It went so far that Rich actually composed a letter of resignation to Mr. Cooke, which asked how Mr. Cooke expected him to sell shmoo advertising since he knew nothing about selling advertising or shmoos.

A few days after I started the prank, I called Rich at home to let him in on the joke.

"Rich, you know those shmoos?" I began.

"Yes," he replied despondently.

"Well, I was only kidding," I confessed.

There was silence as he processed the news.

"What?" he shouted.

"I was only kidding about the shmoos."

Silence.

"Oh, I'm so happy," Rich said. "You son of a bitch. ...Oh, I am so relieved. ... You son of a bitch."

I think we sold him on the prank because even years later Rich and I still laugh about it. And luckily for me, he never sent Mr. Cooke that resignation letter.

3

SECOND PERIOD

JESTER'S TALES IN THE KINGS' COURT

AIRSICKNESS

Pete Weber, my broadcast partner from 1979 to 1981, liked to pull some practical jokes. On an early-morning commercial flight out of Boston, Pete had a window seat, and I was on the aisle of a fully loaded plane. In those years, nearly all teams used commercial flights. A gentleman we didn't know was seated between us. I was reading the morning newspaper as Pete leaned forward and said to me, "Boy, I sure hope I don't get sick like I did on the last flight."

With that, I looked at our fellow passenger, and he had his head down and was shaking it as if to say, "Why me?"

I said to him, "I'd switch seats with you, but the last flight he threw up all over my pants and shoes."

Now the guy was really upset. As we pushed back from the gate, Pete made a big production out of getting the "barf" bag out of the seat pocket and getting it opened. He leaned his head against the window, and all the time we were taxiing, he pretended as if he were going to be sick. By now our friend is

Bob Miller (right) with Peter Weber–Kings Color Commentator, 1979-1981.
PHOTO COURTESY OF THE LOS ANGELES KINGS

trying to be subtle as he peers over the tops of the seats in front of him to see if there is another open seat. There were none.

All that time, I was holding the newspaper over my face because I was laughing so hard. As we started rolling down the runway for takeoff, Pete, louder than I think he meant to, let out a loud sound as if he were vomiting—so loud that a woman with a huge bouffant hairdo seated in front of him let out a scream and threw her arms behind her head envisioning what was coming.

We all had a good laugh, even our unwilling victim in the middle seat.

BOO

One of the funniest incidents at a Kings training camp took place in 1986. The Kings held training camp in Victoria, British Columbia, Canada, and the team was headquartered at the Harbour Towers hotel. The hotel featured balconies outside some rooms, and it was possible, although not easy, to climb from one balcony to the one next door.

It was the night before the end of camp, and curfew was at 10 p.m. Kings players Bernie Nicholls and Phil Sykes decided to climb over to an adjoining balcony on the fifth floor to frighten two French-Canadian junior players who had been invited to camp. Unbeknownst to Nicholls and Sykes, the problem was the two young players had been cut from the roster earlier in the day and sent back to their junior teams.

As Nicholls and Sykes climbed to the balcony of the adjoining room, they found the sliding-glass door open, as it was a pleasant fall night in Victoria. Nicholls was the first to enter the room, bursting through the curtains, racing over to the bed and screaming, "Yaaaaaah!" Right behind him was Sykes who also raced to the bed screaming.

A hotel prank cost Bernie Nicholls $500 in Kangaroo Court. *PHOTO COURTESY OF THE LOS ANGELES KINGS*

At this point, two elderly women, who now occupied the room, sat bolt upright in bed and also started screaming. Sykes later said, "That scared us out of our minds." They both bolted to the balcony and back to Nicholls' room.

Nicholls' roommate was Kings defenseman Dean Kennedy. The next morning word of the prank got around, and Kings coach Pat Quinn was fuming. At practice, Sykes said Quinn skated the team hard and all the while stood at center ice, with a scowl on his face, slamming the blade of his stick onto the ice. Quinn thought Kennedy was one of the culprits since he roomed with Nicholls. Quinn was so upset at the two players he wouldn't call them by name; he called them by their numbers—

Peter Weber—Kings Color Commentator, 1979-1981.
PHOTO COURTESY OF THE NASHVILLE PREDATORS

No. 9 and No. 6. At the end of practice, Quinn said, "Nine and six, I want to see you." Sykes told No. 6, Dean Kennedy, "I'll go talk to him." Quinn looked at Sykes and said, "What are you doing here?" Sykes said, "Well, I was involved in what I think you want to talk to us about."

Nicholls and Sykes recounted the story, and when they got to the part about the elderly ladies screaming and scaring Nicholls and Sykes, Quinn had to smile. After the incident, the two ladies had called the front desk, and Nicholls and Sykes had to pay for the ladies' room and their incidental expenses. A Kings players' "Kangaroo Court" fined Nicholls and Sykes $500, which was contributed to the players' Halloween party fund.

THE RACE

Practical jokes are a part of any sports team, and the Kings have had their share. On the 1973 Kings team was a player named Don Kozak, who prided himself in maintaining superb physical condition. He and his wife, Tanya, lived in an area of Los Angeles called the Palos Verdes Peninsula and during the summer months Tanya would ride her horse through the hills of Palos Verdes while he ran behind her for miles. He would also run on the beach for several miles a day to get in shape.

One September day at the Victoria training camp, the Kings players decided to pull a joke on Kozak and bet him that goaltender Rogie Vachon could beat him in a race. Vachon, although a tremendous goaltender, was never known for exercising too strenuously. The players all put up phony bets, and the race was on. Behind the Memorial Arena in Victoria was a huge rock—so big that the entire team could stand on it and so high that you couldn't see one side from the other. The race was to consist of 10 laps around the rock. Each runner had a trainer, Real Lemieux was Kozak's trainer; and Gilles Marotte was the trainer for Vachon. All of the players except Kozak were

Rogie Vachon is the winningest goalie in Kings history, with 171 victories from 1971 to 1978. *PHOTO BY WEN ROBERTS PHOTOGRAPHY*

in on the ruse, and Lemieux instructed Kozak to "… take off like a rabbit and Vachon would never catch up."

The Kings had a player on that team named Randy Rota, who was about the same size and build as Vachon. They dressed Rota and Vachon alike, and when the race started, Vachon allowed Kozak to sprint out ahead. When he was out of sight, Vachon left the track and hid in the bushes, and Rota took his place the track. Rota stayed far enough behind that when Kozak looked over his shoulder, he thought it was Vachon. Prior to the final lap, Vachon in the weeds, splashed water on himself, came back on the track, and sprinted to overtake Kozak, who couldn't believe that Rogie had that much stamina left. As Vachon started to pass Kozak in the final turn, Kozy, who was stumbling and exhausted, started grabbing Vachon's shirt and holding him up. Rogie pulled away, however, and won the race, much to the dismay of Kozak. Here he had trained all summer and was in tip-top shape and couldn't even beat Vachon. Kozy was in tears, and the players started paying up their phony bets.

So distraught and exhausted was Kozak that he missed practice that morning; but after a while, the players let him in on the practical joke.

EIGHT INCHES OF SHAFT

Sometimes things you say on the air don't come out the way you intend them to. The night of March 21, 1981, the Kings were playing in Edmonton. At one point in the game, Kings goaltender Mario Lessard broke his stick. A goalie is the only player who can continue to play with a broken stick; and in my excitement calling the play-by-play, I said, "Mario Lessard has broken his stick …" and here's when I realized this was not going to sound right, "… he's standing in front of the net with about eight inches of his shaft in his hand."

Mario Lessard holds the Kings record for most wins in a season—35 in 1980-81.
PHOTO COURTESY OF THE LOS ANGELES KINGS

My broadcast partner, Pete Weber, was howling, and I later told Mario that I had given him the benefit of the doubt.

PEEING IN PHILLY

At the Spectrum in Philadelphia, the broadcast location was at the top of the upper deck, and no bathroom facilities were available. During the third period of a game on November 3, 1985, I was in trouble. Nature was calling, and I was extremely uncomfortable. The scoreboard clock showed about eight minutes left, which meant in real time about 15 minutes; and we still had a postgame show to do. I realized I couldn't make it that long and that I would have to join a long list of announcers who, during their careers, were forced to use the soft-drink cups to relieve themselves. I knew I couldn't do it during a stoppage in play—if my partner Nick Nickson ever saw me, we would both break up in fits of laughter. As Nick was talking, I lined up the soft-drink cup; and as I did the play-by-play, I started urinating into the cup. A further problem occurred in that one cup was not enough. So I had to stop, lean down, and with my head on the counter, line up another cup, all the while saying, "The face-off is in the Kings zone …" etc.

I managed to pull it off, and only at the end of the game did I tell Nick what I had done. To this day, I'm not sure he believes me.

CONFUSED BUSES, LOST DRIVERS

Team-bus drivers often are the targets of visiting coaches and players. Two such incidents took place in the mid-1970s in Boston, which is an awful place to drive. It's amazing to me how bus drivers and taxi drivers in that city sometimes have no idea of directions.

Kings coach Bob Pulford sat on the bus where most coaches sit—the front seat on the opposite side of the driver. In this instance, it was becoming apparent the driver was not sure how to get to the Boston Garden, so Pulford started giving him directions. In his usual gruff voice Pulford said, "Turn right; now take a left; now turn right again." We ended up with the bus in a dead-end alley. The players were stifling laughs, as they knew Pulford was embarrassed.

The driver slowly turned in his seat to face Pulford and said, "Have you got any other bright ideas?"

Pulford, with his head down, mumbled, "Well, you're on your own now."

As a player and as a Kings coach, Bob Berry took his cue from Pulford on how to berate bus drivers. One late night—again in Boston during his playing career—Berry was seated right behind the driver with a hanging garment bag separating the two. Most of the players were sleeping when it became obvious the second time we circled the Boston Garden, that the driver didn't know the way to the hotel. Soon a voice from the rear of the bus said, "Hey, Bussie, we're going to be in town for two days. We don't need a tour at two in the morning."

Berry was calmly reading a book and soon the players started egging him on. Defenseman Bob Murdoch was yelling, "Hey, Bobby Berry, are you okay? Are you sick? Hey, Berry, we're lost. Are you sleeping?"

All the while Berry just smiled to himself, said nothing, and kept reading.

Finally, the driver found the hotel; and as he pulled up in front and stopped the bus, Berry calmly pulled the garment bag aside and said to the driver, "You f——ing dummy."

The players broke up laughing.

***

One bus driver who captured the support of the Kings players was a young black man in Detroit named Wade.

The year was 1975 and the Kings had played in Pittsburgh on November 22 and lost 6-3. Immediately after the game, they flew to Detroit, arriving at about 1 a.m. and not in a good mood. Usually the driver simply starts driving, but this night the driver stood up in of the bus and said, "Gentlemens, welcome to Detroit. My name is Wade, and I'll be your driver during your stay here." At this point, the annoyed players hollered, "Just drive the bus." Wade smiled and as he started to pull away, he happened to grind the gears as he shifted. All the players started laughing, and so did Wade.

The game in Detroit on November 23 was Marcel Dionne's first appearance back in Detroit against the team he left to join the Kings. A raucous standing-room-only crowd of 14,565 filled the old Olympia Stadium. They hung derisive banners and booed Dionne all night long. Fans behind the Kings bench threw programs and paper cups filled with beer and soft drinks at Kings coach Bob Pulford. Pulford and Kings players almost went into the stands after a couple of fans; and police even ejected one fan. Detroit won the game 4-1.

Olympia Stadium had a lobby area where players could greet family and friends after the game. That night police informed the Kings that no one in the Kings party would be allowed into the lobby due to security problems. All team personnel were told to leave the locker room through a back door leading to the parking lot. The team bus pulled up close enough to the door so that when the bus doors were opened, no one could get past the bus doors to the locker-room door as hundreds of unruly fans were mulling over a riot in the parking lot.

As the Kings' bus started to pull away, two crazed, drunken Red Wings fans defiantly stood about 20 feet away in front of the bus. Wade floored the gas pedal and went right at the two, who leaped out of the way. The players were now cheering Wade with shouts of "Way to go, Wade!" and "Let's hear it for Wade!"

Wade made a lot of friends on that Kings team.

KANSAS CITY SCOUTS

In 1974, the Kansas City Scouts entered the National Hockey League. They played in Kansas City for two years then moved to Denver as the Colorado Rockies from 1976 to 1982; and later moved to New Jersey as the Devils.

The Scouts were not a good team and won only 12 games in the 1975-76 season (in an 80-game schedule). On the night of March 30, 1976, they were in the midst of a long losing streak when they met the Los Angeles Kings in Kansas City. The Scouts jumped out to a 3-0 lead just 8:21 into the first period. I couldn't believe the Kings were playing so poorly against a bad team. With just one second left in the first period, Kings defenseman Larry Brown scored to make it 3-2, and the Kings were back in the game. At the end of the second period Kansas City led 6-5.

At one point in the third period, as the Kings made a comeback, the Kansas City fans became upset and started littering the ice with programs and soft-drink cups. In Kemper Arena, our broadcast location was an open suite at the back of the lower level of seats with the fans seated right in front of us. At that point, I said on the air, "Well, this shows us the mentality of these fans, stupidly littering the ice with debris."

It was then I heard a deep, gruff voice coming from about eight rows in front of us, "Did you hear what he said about us?" a Scouts fans was asking other fans seated near him.

With that, the fan stood up, all six feet, five inches of him. He started toward the broadcast booth—not coming up the aisle but stepping over the backs of seats. We had a low Plexiglas barrier in front of us, and the fan leaned on that and stared at me from about a foot away. I thought he was going to pick up a soft drink I had and throw it at me. My partner, Dan Avey, was twirling his handheld microphone, ready to bop the guy over the head if he tried anything. All this time, the game was being played, and I had to look around the fan to call the play-by-play. I was determined not to let him interrupt my concentration; and when the Kings' Tommy Williams scored his third goal of the game to give the Kings the lead, I really poured it on—just to upset the fan even more. By this time, the fan was spitting mad. In his frustration, he tore his ticket stub into shreds and threw them at me, then said, "I'll see *you* later."

When all of this started, Avey told a little female security guard to go for help. If I saw her today, it would be the first time since she left the booth—she simply disappeared and never returned. You could enter our booth from the concourse, so I spent the rest of the game alternating between watching the game and peering over my shoulder to see if my "friend" would return. He never showed.

Oh, yes … the Kings won the game 8-6.

REBECCA CARBINO

One night in the mid-1990s, the Kings were in Hartford to play the Whalers. In the game notes, the national anthem singer is always identified, and this night the notes said the singer would be Rebecca Carbino. Our television producer told me when to announce the anthem, and I said, "Now, ladies and gentlemen, from Hartford, Connecticut, here is Rebecca Carbino with our national anthem."

As I looked down on the ice, I saw a 6-foot-5, heavyset black man making his way on the ice to sing the anthem. He had a beautiful, deep voice and did a superb job. Usually, my partner, Jim Fox, is the first one to speak on the air following the anthem, but this night, all during the anthem, he was laughing and pointing at me as if to say, "You've got to get yourself out of this one."

When the anthem was over and we came back on the air, I said, "Ladies and gentlemen, I'm not from Hartford—and I don't know Rebecca Carbino—but that was *not* her."

TWO WEEKS

The Kings had a disastrous season in 1983-84, winning just 23 games, good for a mere 59 points and fifth place in the Smythe Division.

Nick Nickson—Kings Color Commentator, 1981-1990. Nick currently does Kings radio play-by-play. *PHOTO BY ANDREW BERNSTEIN, COURTESY OF THE LOS ANGELES KINGS*

The frustration for me reached its peak in late February. On February 28, the Kings were embarrassed in Calgary 9-1. They were in the midst of a 10-game losing streak. Ten games later, on March 17 in Edmonton, the Kings trailed the Oilers 8-1 when Edmonton's Glenn Anderson scored with 1:45 left in the game and I disgustedly said on the air, "It's now 9 to 1. I haven't seen the Kings play this bad in, oh … two weeks."

My partner, Nick Nickson, howled with laughter. He said he thought I was going to say something like 20 years, not two weeks. Nick left the booth, and I could hear him howling out in the hallway. I could barely speak due to laughing. There was no play-by-play for about the final 90 seconds of the game.

ROOM SERVICE, ANYONE?

At the 1974 NHL All-Star Game in Chicago, Dan Avey pulled a practical joke on Kings publicity director Mike Hope. We were staying at the Palmer House hotel in downtown Chicago; and when we checked in, Avey switched the rooms of general manager Jake Milford and Hope. Hope got the suite intended for Milford, and Milford got the tiny room reserved for Hope. Avey then called the hotel catering service and ordered two plates of hors d'oeuvres, including chocolate-covered strawberries, to be sent to Hope's suite. Hope was under the impression that all this was free—compliments of the hotel. He called me and said, "You've got to come here and see my room; and the hotel is sending me free food."

Hope was on the trip to help legendary *Los Angeles Times* columnist, Jim Murray, who wanted to interview the Blackhawks' Stan Mikita. Soon, we had a roomful of people in Hope's suite enjoying the food and drinks.

Milford arrived all upset because Hope had a bigger room than he did, not aware that Avey had switched the rooms.

Dan Avey—Kings Color Commentator, 1969-1976. *PHOTO COURTESY OF KABC RADIO*

Milford complained his room was so small he had to go into the hallway just to change his mind. All this time, Avey was calling room service to send up more food. Some of us were in on the prank, and we were enjoying that Hope was thinking how wonderful it was that he was receiving this type of hospitality from the hotel.

Avey approved the hotel bills in those days so everything was handled without Jack Kent Cooke's knowledge.

HAWAIIAN REWARDS

In 1980-81, the Kings had their third-best season in team history with 99 points. Coach Bob Berry led the Kings to 43 wins and second place in the Norris Division, and fourth best in the NHL overall.

Late in February, owner Jerry Buss promised the Kings he would take the players, their families, and other members of the organization to Hawaii after the playoffs. Well the playoffs had a quick and disappointing end as the Kings lost 3-1 in a best-of-five series with the New York Rangers. The final game was a 10-3 rout in New York. Yet, the Kings were off to Hawaii.

Hours before the plane left, the Kings announced that coach Bob Berry had signed a new contract. A couple of days later in Honolulu, Berry had second thoughts and resigned. Later that summer, he signed as head coach with Montreal, and some felt he had sought that job before the Kings left on the trip.

While staying at the Hilton Hawaiian Village in Honolulu, many of the players and personnel would gather on the beach at Waikiki each morning after breakfast. One morning, Captain Dave Lewis was reading the scores in the morning sports section. All of a sudden, he stopped and said, "Holy cow, some stoops are still playing." Of course, the successful teams were still battling for the Stanley Cup while the Kings relaxed in Hawaii.

HOPE AND BROWN

When I joined the Kings in August 1973, the publicity director for the team was an energetic, feisty little guy named Mike Hope. He was a bundle of energy, jumped right into the job, and wasn't afraid to let his opinions be known to anyone—including owner Jack Kent Cooke or the team's general manager or players.

The Kings had a defenseman in those years named Larry Brown, and Larry's wife, Jeanne, was also his agent. Whenever Larry would get injured in a game, Jeanne would run down to the dressing room to check on the seriousness of the injury. Kings general manager Jake Milford told Hope that he didn't want any wives in the dressing room.

One game, Larry got injured, and Jeanne raced downstairs and entered the locker room. Hope told her she was not welcome and took her by the arm and ushered her out. She was not happy about this situation.

After the second period of that game, Hope and Jeanne met again at the landing of a narrow stairway leading down to the locker room. Hope said to her, "I've told you a dozen times, you can't go into the locker room."

Jeanne replied, "You can't tell me what to do."

Hope said, "I'll have security throw you out."

With that Jeanne hauled off and slapped Hope in the face. Not one to back down, Hope slapped her in the face right back. She started crying, and Hope thought he had gone too far. He went up to find Milford and tell him what had happened, thinking he would be fired. Upon hearing the story, Milford said, "Good ... Larry should have done that a long time ago."

BLOODY BROPHY

On December 1, 1988, a strange and shocking incident took place during a game between the Kings and Toronto Maple Leafs. The Kings won the game 9-3, and Bernie Nicholls had eight points on two goals and six assists.

The shocker came at the start of the third period with the Kings ahead 6-1. At the Forum in L.A., the opposing coach could reach the bench by ducking underneath the stands rather than walking the long way around and access the bench from the ice. Toronto coach John Brophy decided to duck under the stands, but he rose too soon, struck his head on the metal supports, and suffered a deep gash. Brophy had a full head of white hair, and as I looked down from our telecast location, I noticed something red running down the side of his head and under his shirt collar.

I asked the cameraman to get a tight shot; and sure enough, Brophy's head was gushing blood, but he was still coaching as if he were oblivious to what was happening. Soon the hair on the side of his head was bright red, covered in blood, and Toronto players were telling him to go get medical attention. He refused, thinking it would be an inspiration for his team, and they would come back and win the game. Maple Leaf player Mike Allison told me later all the players were laughing at him and rather than taking it as inspiration they were thinking, "This is nuts."

It was only after the game that Brophy would get stitches—33 of them without painkillers to show how tough he was.

STREAKS OF THE STRANGE

In 1974, the "streaking" craze was prevalent, and the Kings were not to be left out. Before a game with the Pittsburgh Penguins at the Forum on March 13, Bryant Gumbel, then a young sportscaster at Channel 4 (KNBC) in Los Angeles, informed me he heard there would be a streaker on the ice some time that night.

I was in the broadcast booth about half an hour before the teams came out for warm-ups, and sure enough, a young lady came onto the ice where the visiting team enters. She was wearing nothing but a pair of sneakers and was holding a Kings pennant above her head. The crowd was startled at first but then cheered as she ran the length of the ice, exited where the Kings enter, jumped into a waiting car in the tunnel, and was whisked away. We found out later she was a stripper named "Miss Cindy" and that Kings owner Jack Kent Cooke, always looking for publicity, had approved paying her $100 to streak.

***

One other night, March 5, 1988, at the Forum, someone threw a live chicken on the ice in the first period as the game was in progress. The chicken had what looked like a blue cloth napkin on its back, and it was so scared it remained motionless as it soiled the ice. To my disbelief, play continued for about 30 seconds; and Kings players were skating and stick-handling around the chicken until the referee stopped play. Finally the chicken was removed.

***

Prior to the start of each NHL game, the public address announcer warns spectators to be alert because the puck can fly into the stands and cause injury. One night at the Forum, to my left, a hard slap shot was fired just over the glass and into the crowd. I saw a woman grab her head with both hands, and I thought she had been hit in the forehead and injured. At that point, however, all the fans seated near her started laughing.

The Kings met the New York Rangers in a preseason outdoor game at Caesar's Palace in Las Vegas. *PHOTO BY ANDREW BERNSTEIN, COURTESY OF THE LOS ANGELES KINGS*

It so happened the woman was wearing a wig, and the puck had picked the wig off her head and knocked it about eight rows behind her. She was covering her hair in embarrassment while the crowd passed the wig down the rows back to her.

VEGAS ICE

Usually the only thing to get excited about in the preseason is that it signals the regular season is near, but it's also a chance to see some young prospects in game situations. The Kings changed that in 1991, when they uniquely scheduled an outdoor game at Caesar's Palace in Las Vegas against the New York Rangers.

The game was played on a portable ice rink set up in the parking lot behind the hotel, where boxing matches were held. To shield the ice from the sun, netting held up by ropes was positioned about 10 feet above the ice. At 1 p.m. on game day, workmen removing the net accidentally dropped it on the ice, and the heated ropes melted into the ice causing hundreds of ripples on the surface. Then, about 1:30, it rained for half an hour.

At 4:30, 1 walked to the rink and watched a maintenance man squeegee about an inch of water off the ice. I thought, "There is no way a game will be played tonight." Fortunately, the portable ice is quite thick, and the Zamboni machine was able to scrape off the ripples and reflood the ice as the temperature was dropped. Sure enough, by 7:30 that night, 13,007 fans, all decked out in various NHL team jerseys, were ready for the opening face-off with the temperature at 85 degrees.

Kings goalie Kelly Hrudey consented—and so did the NHL—to have a tiny television camera taped to the side of his helmet. We called it the "Hrudey Cam," and it may have been the first point-of-view camera used in hockey. It was supposed to give the television viewer the same perspective of the play as the goalie. At one point, one of the officials skated toward Hrudey, looked at his helmet, and mouthed the words "Hi, Mom!" into the camera.

Another problem that night was grasshoppers. Attracted by the bright lights, they were all over the ice. They were about an inch and a half long, and players would cut them in half as they skated over them.

The Kings won the game 5-2, and the fans had a great time at the game and in the casinos. The next day, the Kings flew all the way across country to Charlotte, North Carolina, to play the Rangers on September 29, but the portable ice at the Charlotte Coliseum was chipping, and the game was cancelled due to the poor ice conditions.

HOT NEWS

One Sunday morning in 1974, when the Kings' charter bus was leaving the Vancouver airport, Don Kozak was sitting in front of Kings radio and television-color commentator Dan Avey, engrossed in reading the newspaper. Kozak had pulled out one section and left the rest of the paper in the aisle between his seat and the seat of Kings trainer Pete Demers. While Kozak caught up on the news, Avey took a matchbook from his pocket, got out a match, and lit it. As quick as lightning Avey reached between the seats and set the bottom edge of Kozak's paper on fire. The little flame grew and began spitting out smoke, but Kozak was so wrapped up in his reading that he didn't notice.

A few moments later, his eyes zeroed in on the flames and the smoke; and he tossed the paper across the aisle and onto Demers' head. Demers, who is jittery even in the best of times, let out this blood-curdling scream and dropped the section where the rest of the Sunday paper sat, setting it ablaze, and ran to the front of the bus. The fire grew, reaching the armrests as the furious driver pulled to the side of the road and searched for the key to unlock the fire extinguisher. I wasn't going to stand around; I got off the bus and waited with assistant trainer John Holmes on the side of the road.

Back on the bus, Avey, who started the whole escapade, jumped on the paper and stomped the fire out with his feet.

Meanwhile, Holmes and I were enjoying a smoke-free environment when Coach Bob Pulford leaned out of the door.

"Get the hell back in the bus," he ordered gruffly.

"Pully, the bus is on fire," I stated. "I think I'll stand out here if you don't mind."

As we returned to our seats, I heard the team laughing hysterically. The driver got up in the front of the bus and began to chew them out.

"You think this is a joke," he ranted. "You call yourselves professionals. There's going to be a bill for the fire damage to this vehicle."

The players were less than sympathetic.

"Sit down and drive the f---ing bus," one of them hollered.

I wish I could say that was a one-time incident. However, on February 28, 1977, we had another hot news flash in Buffalo. The Kings had played the Sabres the night before, and we were headed to the airport for an early-morning flight to Washington D.C. It was about 6:00 a.m., and all was quiet with most of the players and personnel asleep.

All of a sudden, goaltender Rogie Vachon began yelling from the back, in his French-Canadian accent, "Stop de bus! Stop de bus!"

When I looked back there, the entire back of the bus was red with flames. The driver pulled over and was steaming mad. Before he got back there, someone had stomped out another newspaper fire.

"Y-y-you g-g-guys t-t-think t-t-this is f-f-funny?" he stuttered from the front of the bus. "Y-y-you c-c-call y-y-yourselves p-p-professionals."

And once again, one of the players responded.

"Just drive the f---ing bus."

He dropped us off and all of the team—except Coach Pulford—continued to the terminal. Once we got there, I waited to speak to the coach. After a very long time, he finally showed up.

"What took you so long?"

"The driver swore he would not pick us up for the game next week," Pulford answered. We were playing Buffalo a few days later to make up a cancelled game. "It took some tickets to the game and a promise that no one would set his bus on fire to change his mind."

I just shook my head and hoped that Pulford could make sure that he'd uphold his end of the bargain.

TIME TO KILL IN PHILLY

Things don't always go smoothly on the road, especially back in the days when teams took commercial travel. On Saturday, January 6, 1979, the Kings won in Pittsburgh and were scheduled to take an early-morning Sunday flight to Philadelphia for a game that night. Halfway through the flight the pilot announced that due to ice and snow we would be diverted to New York and would not land in Philadelphia. The team had to scramble to obtain a chartered bus, and about 2 p.m., we headed for Philadelphia on snow-covered roads. Upon arriving, there was no time to check into the team's hotel, so they went right to The Spectrum, home of the Flyers.

The game against the Flyers was to start at 7 p.m. We were in the midst of a live pregame show on television when it was announced that, due to a gymnastics meet in the building that afternoon, the ice was not ready, and the game would be delayed until 7:30.

So, there we were on live television with a half hour to fill on the spur of the moment. If we had been told at noon that we had to fill a half hour, we probably would have panicked, but on short notice your brain kicks into gear, and you think of all kinds of things to say. My partner, Pete Weber, and I talked about the game, the Kings, the season so far, we interviewed Flyers announcer Gene Hart, and all of a sudden, the half hour was gone.

While I was looking at the camera during our fill time, I noticed in my peripheral vision something flash past to my left. It wasn't until we went to a break that the cameraman said, "Did you see the size of that rat?" A huge rat had scurried along one of our television cables. After hearing that, I was glad I hadn't seen it.

By the way, the travel-weary Kings lost the game that night 3-0.

BUFFALO SNOW

Buffalo, New York, is known for sudden snowstorms, and one hit the area on January 10, 1982. The Kings hotel was only about a quarter-mile from the Auditorium. Some players decided to walk to the game, but halfway there they were hit with a horrendous storm.

The snow was so bad that even though over 15,000 tickets had been sold, only 2,079 brave souls made it to the game—the smallest crowd in Sabres history. The visibility was so bad that some people had to abandon their cars on a bridge behind the arena and be led off the bridge holding onto ropes. The wind chill was 50 below zero. During the game, the Sabres announced that fans who were stranded were welcome to spend the night in the Auditorium and the Sabres offices. The next morning a picture in the Buffalo newspaper showed a fan sleeping overnight in the penalty box.

After the game, Kings players and team personnel were told that four-wheel-drive vehicles would take them back to the hotel. There was only one vehicle, and it was taking four people at a time. The short roundtrip was taking 45 minutes. When I got there, I found about 30 people in line ahead of me, so I decided to walk. I used my broadcast headphones as earmuffs and started in the general direction of the hotel. Halfway to the hotel in a blinding snowstorm, I thought I wasn't going to make it. I was walking in the street and decided I'd better get on the sidewalk in case a snowplow came along. If that happened, I figured they wouldn't find me until the next May.

When I finally made it to the hotel, I discovered a quarter-size area of skin on my face that looked like the beginning of frostbite, but at least I made it back to the bar for "last call."

SNOW IN ST. LOUIS

You would expect snow to be a problem in Buffalo, New York, but not in St. Louis. On December 19, 1973, the Kings were in St. Louis to play the Blues, but a snowstorm held the crowd to only 4,115.

We were doing our radio pregame show when I heard a public address announcement. I had earphones on and couldn't make out the announcement, but all of a sudden, the fans started rushing for the exits. I thought to myself, "Maybe the announcer said the building was on fire." When we broke for a commercial, I asked our engineer what the announcement was to the crowd. He said they told fans that since they had made an effort to battle the storm and attend the game, there would be free beer and hot dogs at the concession stands.

The next morning, the Kings were to fly home, but due to the storm, all flights were cancelled or delayed. In those days, the radio-television color commentator, Dan Avey, also handled the team travel arrangements. While Dan manned the phones at the hotel looking for a flight, I headed for the airport about 9 a.m.

We didn't get out of St. Louis until 6 p.m. that night, so I spent all day in the TWA lounge. I struck up a conversation with a gentleman who said he was trying to get to Anaheim, California, for a concert. I asked his name, and he said, "I'm Tex Beneke, the leader of the Glenn Miller orchestra."

CALGARY TOWER

At the start of the 1990 playoffs in Calgary, I received a phone call one morning from Bob Borgen, our television feature producer. He said, "How would you like to do a feature from the top of the Calgary Tower?"

The Calgary Tower is a 625-foot-high landmark in downtown Calgary with a restaurant and observation deck on top. I said, "You mean in the restaurant?" and he replied, "No, I mean out on the roof of the tower."

He told me I would be hooked to a safety belt, but then he added—jokingly, I hoped—"If you fall to your death, your family will receive free season tickets to the Flames games."

I thought it might be fun, so I agreed. I signed a release with Tower management and climbed through a trap door out onto the roof, looking straight down to the street some 625 feet below. The roof was slanted toward the outside edge, so I walked on a slight incline uphill toward a television antenna in the middle of the roof. At this point, I saw a television cameraman setting up his tripod.

Bob Miller and television producer Bob Borgen on top of the 625-foot Calgary (Alberta) Tower. *PHOTO COURTESY OF BOB BORGEN*

I did a commentary on the series, which featured the Kings against the defending Stanley Cup Champion Calgary Flames. Borgen then said for me to remain on top of the Tower until he and the camera crew could drive to the far side of the Saddledome. With a zoom lens, they'd get a shot toward the arena, then over the arena to the top of the tower. At that point, they would flash the headlights on their van, and I would then raise a Kings pennant over my head to signify the Kings were on top of Calgary.

The following day, Randy Hahn, who was the third announcer on our crew and who did the between-periods features, was out with a television crew at the Calgary Olympic ski-jump site. As a joke, with the crew taping, Randy went to a high-powered binocular stand and looked through the binoculars, then turned toward the camera and said, "Wow, some asshole is standing on top of the Calgary Tower." At that point, they were going to cut to me with the pennant above my head. Fortunately, that portion never got on the air.

COATES PENALTY

The referee doesn't usually penalize publicity men, but it happened on January 25, 1979, at the Forum in a game between the Kings and the Detroit Red Wings. The Kings were leading 6-1 near the end of the second period when the Red Wings got two penalties at 17:18 and were two men short, then got another at 18:20. At the end of the period, Detroit received a bench minor at the 20-minute mark.

When the third period started, none of us knew what the bench penalty was for and neither did anyone at the penalty timekeeper's bench. It was later discovered that, Detroit's director of publicity, Al Coates, was so incensed at the officiating that he charged to the referees' locker room at the end of the second period and was waiting for referee Ron Wicks to come off the ice. Coates said he grabbed the referee around the shoulders and neck, but two policemen intervened and half-dragged, half-escorted him to the Detroit locker-room area, asking Red Wings personnel, "Does anyone know this guy?" When he was identified, he was released.

Coates later got a call of reprimand from NHL President John Ziegler, and he phoned Wicks to apologize for his actions as well. The Red Wings rallied for three goals in the third period, and the game ended tied 6-6.

The brash young Coates cooled off, though, and went on to become a high-ranking executive with the Calgary Flames and now with the Mighty Ducks of Anaheim.

BLOWOUT

On January 13, 1991, the Kings flew East for road games in New Jersey, Hartford, and Boston. It proved to be a very painful road trip for me as shortly after we arrived in New Jersey I started having a problem with hemorrhoids.

After the game in New Jersey on January 14, the Kings boarded a bus for the short trip to Hartford, Connecticut. By game day, January 16, it was painful for me to walk. I alerted my partner, Jim Fox, about the problem just in case something happened, and I couldn't complete the telecast. I remember that was the night the Gulf War started, and I said I was firing some scud missiles of my own. I made it through that game and then endured a painful two-hour bus ride to Boston.

My seat partner on the bus was Kings trainer Pete Demers, and he could see I was in discomfort. When we arrived at Boston about 1 a.m., Pete set out to find an all-night pharmacy. He brought me some Epsom salts and told me to soak in the bathtub. Hours later the hemorrhoid was getting worse. I had not slept, and we had a telecast that night.

About 7 a.m., I started looking in the Yellow Pages for a doctor. I saw an ad for an outpatient clinic at Massachusetts General Hospital with no appointment needed. I took a taxi to the hospital where the intern examining me said, "I can't handle this, and I need to get some help." He summoned a doctor, who told me I needed surgery as soon as possible. I asked him if I could do a telecast that night and then fly to L.A. With some trepidation, he said that I could if I got a donut pillow to sit on and took some painkillers. He then called my doctor in Los Angeles and informed him of the situation.

I made it through the game and the six-hour flight home. I was probably taking a huge risk, since something could have ruptured during the flight. My wife met me at the airport at 4 a.m., and we went straight to the hospital. The doctor said he had watched us on camera during the telecast, and he said, "I couldn't believe you were upbeat and smiling with the pain you were experiencing."

I later found out the hemorrhoid was about the size of a baseball. I call it "The Night My Ass Blew Out in Boston."

SECOND INTERMISSION

GEORGE MAGUIRE

George Maguire, the Kings general manager from 1977 to 1983 was a stocky, florid-faced Canadian. He liked to drink a little—or perhaps a lot—and he was an individual who was not happy unless he was upset about something, and the smallest thing could put him in a bad mood. Come to think of it, most of the time he was in a bad mood. He could be belligerent, quarrelsome, combative, coarse, caustic, vulgar, crude, rude, and uncouth—and that was on a good day. I think that just about sums him up. If you need a visual image, just think of the late Australian actor Leo McKern as Horace Rumpole in the English television series *Rumpole of the Bailey*.

He spent 26 years in the Canadian Military, which I think helped shape his personality. He spent years as a scout for the Montreal Canadiens, the Boston Bruins, and the Minnesota North Stars; and as the Chief Scout for the Kings, and he was extremely efficient in that role. When the Kings had traded away most of their high draft picks in the early years, Maguire found some outstanding players that other teams had overlooked, such as Butch Goring (drafted 51st); Neil Komadoski (48th); Dave Hutchison (36th), Gary Sargent (48th), Dave Taylor (210th), and Hall of Fame goalie Billy Smith (59th).

He was brought to L.A. to be assistant general manager to Jake Milford. Owner Jack Kent Cooke had this penchant for pitting two executives against each other until one of them quit; I never understood this type of management. In the summer of 1977, both Milford and head coach Bob Pulford resigned because neither of them could get along with Cooke or with Maguire, who then was named general manager.

I never realized how crazy things could get in professional sports until one night before a home game: Maguire came to my office and told me and my broadcast partner, Rich Marotta, not to mention the name of Bob Murdoch. Murdoch was a Kings defenseman. I asked Maguire, "Why isn't he playing?" Maguire said, "Well, he is playing."

I said, "Murdoch is playing, but you don't want me to mention his name? What am I supposed to say on the air, 'Folks, I know who has the puck, but I can't tell you'?"

Then George made one of the most unbelievable statements ever, as he said, "I don't know, but I'll tell you one thing: this honesty bullshit has got to stop."

Maguire didn't want Murdoch's name mentioned because Mr. Cooke had moved to Nevada due to his divorce proceeding and would listen to the game on radio. Cooke didn't like Murdoch, and each time he would hear me mention Murdoch's name on the broadcast, Cooke would phone George and give him hell. As I recall, that night Murdoch had a great game, blocking shots, making great defensive plays, and even scoring a goal. Each time I would I would say, "What a great play by Murdoch," I would look at George, and he'd be pounding his fist on the counter.

George Maguire—Kings General Manager, 1977-1983.
PHOTO BY WEN ROBERTS PHOTOGRAPHY INK

***

Maguire sat in the front row of the press box about four seats to my right. He could hear us doing the play-by-play. One night on the air, I said to my partner, Pete Weber, "I don't see Butch Goring on the ice or on the bench. Do we have any report that he's injured?" "No I haven't heard about any injury," Pete said. George heard this, and being oblivious to live microphones, he leaned over toward us and said, "Butch Goring's got a boil on his arse—that's why he's not playing." Nothing like our audience getting an up-to-the-minute injury report.

***

In many of the Maguire years, Kings attendance was down. On many nights, the Forum was only half-full. One night the Kings goaltender broke his stick and the Kings iced the puck to get a whistle. When play stopped, the building was quiet, and I heard a fan about two sections over to my right holler, "Hey, Maguire. I didn't pay 10 bucks to see this team ice the puck all night." I looked at George, and he was fuming—his face looked like a thermometer getting redder and redder. George then turned in his seat, looked toward where the voice had come from, and hollered back, "What do you want him to do, play goal with his pecker?"

Two sections of fans broke up laughing.

***

There was a female Kings fan who would be half-soused by the end of the first period. She would then follow Maguire through the crowd as he walked toward the stairway to go down to his office. She would be taunting him, "This team stinks; when are they going to win?" or "I'm a season-ticket holder; when are you going to get some good players?" Finally, one night George had had enough. He whirled around and shouted at her, "You can shove your season tickets right up your arse."

"Wonderful, we are having trouble drawing fans, and the GM is insulting them," I thought.

***

At another game, several people in the press box noticed a couple seated in the upper reaches of the Forum known as the colonnade. This couple was getting more and more amorous, and soon most everyone in the press box was following the action—and I don't mean on the ice. Someone pointed out to George what was going on and George said, "Jesus Christ, you'd think if the guy was going to get laid, he'd buy a higher priced seat."

4

THIRD PERIOD

THE KINGDOM

PAID INTERVIEWS

On January 14, 1979, the Kings were in Boston to play the Bruins. In the Boston Garden, the radio-television location was on one side of the ice, and the print media were on the opposite side. I wanted to interview Kings GM George Maguire between periods on our telecast. I saw George across the ice in the press box, so I called the Bruins media relations director, Nate Greenberg. I asked Nate to ask George if he would join us at the end of the first period. Nate called back and said George refused. I didn't think much of it since I figured he was going to meet with Bruins GM Harry Sinden between periods.

The next morning, as we checked in at Boston's Logan airport, Maguire said to me in a belligerent voice, "What would prompt you to make that request last night?" I thought he meant, "Why didn't you ask me yourself instead of having Nate Greenberg do it?"

I told him I wanted to ask him myself but didn't see him until after I had arrived in our broadcast location. George said, "That isn't what I mean."

I said, "Well, what do you mean?"

"I don't get $500 from Zenith," he answered. "Why would I go on with you?" In those days, our players received $500 to put toward merchandise from Zenith for appearing as guests on our telecasts. I couldn't believe my ears. I was very upset, and I said, "That's a horseshit attitude by our general manager that you need to be paid to go on our telecast."

Now George was upset, and as I walked away, he was shouting, "What do you mean, 'it's a horseshit attitude?'" blah, blah, blah. I then told my partner, Pete Weber, "We will never interview Maguire again, I don't care what happens." And we didn't.

By this time, former Kings general manager Jake Milford was the general manager of the Vancouver Canucks. Whenever the Canucks would play the Kings in L.A., we would interview Jake between periods, but we would never interview Maguire. When the interview was over, Milford would stand behind Maguire and say in a loud voice to me, "Bob, what do I get for being on with you?," and then he would wink at me.

I'd say, loud enough for Maguire to hear, "You get two tailor-made suits from a clothier on Wilshire Boulevard."

Milford would then ask Maguire, "Is that what I get for being on the air?"

Maguire would answer, "Don't ask me. Those two bastards never put me on the air."

All of us—except George—would get a big laugh.

THE MONKEY AND THE ORGAN GRINDER

Probably one of the funniest lines ever uttered in a courtroom occurred during the 1978 off-season. That year, the Detroit Red Wings signed Kings goaltender Rogie Vachon as a free agent,

Jake Milford—Kings General Manager, 1974-1977.

and as compensation, the Kings received Detroit forward Dale McCourt. McCourt had a very good rookie year with Detroit, however, and didn't want to leave the team; so he and then-Red Wings GM Ted Lindsay challenged the deal and went to court to block it.

During the court hearing, Kings GM George Maguire took the stand and said about Detroit, "They shouldn't have messed with my goalie." McCourt's attorney asked Maguire why he didn't make an offer to Vachon, to which Maguire replied, "I did, but I made it to his agent."

The attorney then asked, "Why didn't you make the offer to Mr. Vachon?"

"Why would I talk to the monkey when I can talk to the organ grinder?" Maguire responded.

Al Coates was Detroit's public-relations director at that time, and he said the courtroom exploded in laughter upon hearing Maguire's response. Some observers ran out of the room in hysterics, and the court had to call a recess.

When everything was worked out—a year later—McCourt stayed with Detroit, and the Kings were awarded forward Andre St. Laurent and two No. 1 draft picks from the Red Wings as compensation for their signing Vachon.

With those two No. 1 picks, the Kings drafted defenseman Larry Murphy in 1980 and forward Doug Smith in 1981.

A LITTLE PR

In 1983, the Kings decided to hold training camp in Los Angeles instead of going to some distant locale as they had done in the past. The plan was to make the team more accessible to local reporters so they could stir publicity on the upcoming season. The camp would be held at the Kings practice rink in Culver City, and on the first day of camp, the temperature was about 103 degrees. Overnight, one of the compressors, which keeps the ice frozen, broke down; so when the players and media arrived for the first practice session, the ice was almost completely melted. A quick call was made to George Maguire, who was steaming mad when he arrived at the rink. As he stormed into the building, reporter Sam McManus, of the *Los Angeles Times*, who had been assigned to cover the Kings, said to George, "Can I ask you a question?"

George whirled around and said, "Get away from me, you're a goddamn pest."

This was on the first day—so much for media relations.

***

During a team commercial flight one season, I was seated on the plane when Maguire arrived a little late. He was huffing and puffing, sweating and red in the face as he walked down the aisle struggling with his luggage. I could tell he was in his usual bad mood. Just then, one of the female flight attendants said to him in a cheery voice, "May I take your garment bag, sir?"

George turned and said to her, "You can shove my garment bag right up your arse."

What a wonderful representative of the team.

***

In the Stanley Cup playoffs of 1980, the Kings met the New York Islanders with the series starting on Long Island. Maguire did not accompany the team but flew to New York a day later with the team physician, Dr. Vince Carter. As they were seated in the first-class section, the flight attendant asked what they would like to drink. George said, "I'll have a cocktail," and Dr. Carter said, "I'll have orange juice."

With that, Maguire hollered at Dr. Carter, "Why the hell are you flying first class if you're not going to drink?"

WHO SAID KINGS QUIT?

On November 4, 1978, the New York Rangers played in L.A. and soundly beat the Kings 7-3. I was sitting in the press lounge after the game when George Maguire stormed through on the way to his office. I always enjoyed getting George upset—something that was easy to do—so I looked at him and rolled my eyes in disgust over the Kings' performance.

He said to me, "Get Pluto and bring your tape recorder into my office."

For some unknown reason George always called my partner Pete Weber by cartoon names such as Pluto, Bulldog, and Felix. When we arrived in George's office, he said, "Which one of you said the Kings quit? The game was so bad I couldn't bear to watch, so I came to my office and heard one of you say it looks as if the Kings have quit."

I told him I never said that—nor would I *ever* say that—and Pete said he hadn't said anything like that either.

With that, George pointed at a speaker in the ceiling and asked, "Whose voice comes out of that?"

I told him ours did, and he said, "It was right after the Rangers' seventh goal, so play it on your tape recorder."

I played the tape, and there was no reference to the Kings quitting.

George then said, "Well, one of you said it, and I'd better not ever hear it again."

At this point, I was getting upset and said, "I told you neither one of us said anything about the team quitting."

On the drive home, I wondered who would make a statement like that, and I decided it would probably be the opponent's announcers. The next day, I phoned Maguire's assistant, John

Wolf, and asked him to listen to the Rangers videotape of the game to see if he heard that statement.

He called me back and said, "Yes, right after the Rangers' seventh goal, Bill Chadwick, the Rangers color announcer, said, 'It looks as if the Kings have quit.'"

I told John to save the tape. When I arrived at the Forum that day, I called George to the video room because I had something to show him. He asked if it was a horror show, and I said, "Yes, last night's game." When I played the tape, George said, "Yep, that's what I heard."

I then waited for him to say he was sorry for accusing Pete and me. When I heard nothing I said, "George, I think you owe Pete and me an apology for that childish outburst in your office last night."

I wondered if I had gone too far and overstepped my bounds. He stared at me, puffing his cigar, his face getting bright red, and then he shouted, "Well, I *apologize*. What do you think I am, a goddamn Canadian diplomat?"

"George," I said, "that's one thing I know you're not."

TRADE WITH RANGERS

On March 14, 1996, the Kings made a significant trade with the New York Rangers. The Kings sent Marty McSorley, Jari Kurri, and Shane Churla to New York in exchange for Mattias Norstrom, Ian Laperriere, and Ray Ferraro.

The general manager who made the deal was Sam McMaster. One of the Kings scouts phoned McMaster's home and spoke to his wife, Colleen, who didn't follow the team's transactions too closely. Sam wasn't home, so the scout said he had heard the Kings had made a trade that day and asked Colleen whom they acquired.

Colleen said, "I can't remember exactly, but I think we got a department store [Norstrom], a water [Laperriere], and a sports car [Ferraro]."

PEEPHOLE

When Bob Berry was the Kings head coach in the late 1970s and early 1980s, we would stay in a hotel near the St. Louis airport when in town to play the Blues. One night Bob and I headed to the hotel's bar on the top floor. As we were seated at the bar, we noticed many "ladies of the night" in attendance. After a while, Berry decided it was time to call it a night.

"I'm tired," he explained. "I'm going to my room."

"Okay, I am going to stay and finish my beer," I told him.

Shortly after Bob had left, one of the ladies came up to me.

"Hi, are you staying in the hotel?" she purred.

"Yes."

"What's your room number?"

I can honestly say that I picked a room number, not my own, out of thin air.

"I'll see you later," she promised. "My name is Cindy."

When I returned to my room, I wondered if I had given her the room number of anyone with the Kings, so I checked the rooming list. Oh boy, I had given her Berry's room number. The next morning as I boarded the bus to go to the arena for the morning skate, I found Bob.

"Good morning," I said. "How are you?"

"Horseshit," he replied. "You know how tired I was when I left you last night. Well, I took a hot bath and went to bed, and at 2 a.m. someone was pounding on my door."

"Who was it?" I asked, feigning concern.

"Some hooker. She said, 'It's Cindy.' And I said, 'Who?' And she said, 'I met you upstairs.' I said, 'I didn't meet anybody

Bob Berry–Kings Left Wing, 1970-1977; Kings Coach, 1978-1981.
PHOTO COURTESY OF THE LOS ANGELES KINGS

upstairs. Go away!' She replied, 'Yeah, you did. Look tru da peephole, look tru da peephole.' She had her face in front of the peephole in the door. I told her to get the hell out."

"Boy, that's too bad," I muttered as I bit my cheek to keep from laughing. "Did you ever get back to sleep?"

I kept my mouth shut about the entire mishap for a couple of months until we came back to St. Louis, the same hotel, and the same hotel bar.

"I have a confession to make to you," I told him as I looked at my beer.

The second I said those words he knew exactly what I was about to say.

"You son of a bitch," he seethed, "you sent her to my room."

To this day, I don't think he believes me when I tell him I didn't know it was his room number when I gave it to Cindy.

PULFORD

Hall of Famer, Bob Pulford played 16 years in the NHL—14 of those with the Toronto Maple Leafs, where he was a member of four Stanley Cup-winning teams and the last two of his career with the Los Angeles Kings. He was named head coach of the Kings at the start of the 1972-73 season. He had a dour personality around most people, especially the players, but was a more gregarious person once you came to know him and he came to know you. I asked him once why he was always so stern around the players, and he said, "Because I never want them to think I'm not serious about this game."

On January 15, 1974, the Kings were in Montreal to play a great Canadiens team. The Forum in Montreal was a tough place to play, and the success of the team called "The Flying Frenchmen" made it even tougher. That particular game, the Kings were winning 2-1 in the third period when the Kings'

Hockey Hall of Famer Bob Pulford—Kings Player, 1970-1972; Kings Coach, 1972-1977. *PHOTO COURTESY OF THE CHICAGO BLACKHAWKS*

Frank St. Marseille was called for a tripping penalty with 9:13 left in the game. At the same time, Montreal challenged the legality of the stick of Kings goalie Rogie Vachon. Rogie's stick blade was too wide—it had come from the factory that way—so the Kings received another penalty from referee Wally Harris, and the stick boy was told to get Vachon another stick.

Pulford, upset over the situation, followed the boy into the Kings locker room, locked the door, and said, "Sit down and relax. I'm going to have a cigarette."

Meanwhile, in the arena, none of us knew what the delay was; and as the minutes went by, players from both teams came back on the ice to skate and warm up. At this time, the officials were pounding on the Kings' locker-room door, telling Pulford to get the new stick out there and get the game going. Pulford told them he was trying to cut the stick down to the proper size, but the exasperated officials told him to just play with it the way it was.

Pulford's ploy had worked. The Canadiens had lost their momentum. The Kings killed the penalty two men short for two minutes and won the game.

***

On October 10, 1976, the Kings were in Philadelphia to play another fight-filled game with the Flyers, also known as "The Broad Street Bullies." At 16:56 of the first period, a bench-clearing brawl broke out and delayed the game for 21 minutes. During the brawl, an incensed Pulford grabbed linesman John Brown and was shaking him.

All of a sudden Pulford thought, "What am I doing grabbing an official? I'm in real trouble." So then he started smoothing out the linesman's shirt. Pulford was ejected, becoming the first NHL coach to be ejected from a game since Toe Blake of Montreal was ejected on December 13, 1967, in Boston. The league fined

Pulford an "exorbitant" amount of $350. Pulford had no assistant coaches in those days, so general manager Jake Milford took over behind the bench. The Flyers won the game 1-0.

The referees gave 127 minutes in penalties in the first period, and a second bench-clearing brawl took place in the second period. The NHL assessed $9,750 in fines to the two teams.

***

Pulford's wife, Roslyn, should be credited for a rule that now appears in the NHL rulebook. One day she asked her husband, "When you pull the goalie for an extra attacker, why not have him place his stick across the mouth of the goal; since most empty-net goals are scored on shots where the puck stays down on the ice?"

So in Philadelphia one night, Pulford told goalie Rogie Vachon to leave his stick across the empty net if he was pulled from the game. When the time came, Vachon was trying to break his stick and leave it, but he couldn't break it, so he left the entire stick in front of the goal. Pulford said players on the Flyers bench were going wild, screaming, "That's illegal!" at the referee.

There was no rule against it at that time, but it is now deemed illegal.

NEILSON

In the 1983-84 season, Don Perry was fired as Kings head coach after winning only 14 of 50 games, and after general manager Rogie Vachon coached two games in the interim, the Kings hired Roger Neilson as head coach on January 30, 1984. Neilson had coached Vancouver earlier that season and thus became the second man in history to be head coach of two NHL teams in the same season. Fred Glover was the first at Oakland and L.A. in 1971-72.

Roger Neilson—Kings coach for 28 games in 1984.
PHOTO BY ANDREW BERNSTEIN, COURTESY OF THE LOS ANGELES KINGS

Neilson was known as "Captain Video" because he was the first NHL coach to rely on videotape as a coaching tool. While with the Kings he told me one of the funniest stories and one of the funniest lines I've ever heard from a coach.

While coaching junior hockey at Peterborough, Ontario, his team played the Sault Ste. Marie Greyhounds and were beaten soundly, something like 9-1. The Greyhounds had a mechanical dog at the roof of the building, and every time they would score, someone would release a lever and the dog would go yelping across the arena. Roger said, "We were sick and tired of hearing that dog, so the next time we played there we went to a hardware store and got some chain, a padlock, and some grease. We got into the arena the night before the game, chained and padlocked the dog, and then spread grease on the ladder leading to the dog."

Then Roger had the greatest line I've ever heard from a coach. He said, "That night, we could hardly wait for them to score."

When the Greyhounds did score, an attendant pulled the lever, and the dog vibrated but couldn't move. The attendant then slid down the greased ladder as he tried to get to the dog. "We were losing," Roger said, "but we were in stitches laughing on the bench."

DON'T DANCE

An event occurred on January 24, 1982, that got the Kings some unwanted national attention. The Kings played to a 5-5 tie in Vancouver that night, and all during the game, the Canucks were physically going after Marcel Dionne. At 18:25 of the second period, a fracas broke out, and the Kings' Jay Wells and Vancouver's Ron Delorme fought. Delorme had gone to the penalty box but came back to the ice, and the Kings were outnumbered. Paul Mulvey was on the Kings bench and hadn't

Don Perry—Kings Coach, 1982-1984. PHOTO COURTESY OF THE LOS ANGELES KINGS

played much to that point, but coach Don Perry told him to "get out there and don't dance."

Four times Perry ordered Mulvey off the bench, and it was clear that Perry wanted Mulvey to join the fight. Mulvey hesitated and didn't leave the bench as Mark Hardy and Rick Chartraw jumped off the Kings bench and onto the ice to join the battle.

In the Kings locker room between periods, a major confrontation took place between Perry and Mulvey. Perry threw a skate at Mulvey, but Mulvey's only response was verbal. Perry told the media the story after the game and also told Mulvey he was no longer wanted on the team. Mulvey cleared waivers and was sent to the Kings' minor-league affiliate in New Haven, Connecticut. Perry was interviewed on several national morning television news shows to tell his side of the story. On February 3, the NHL suspended Perry for 15 days and fined the Kings $5,000 for actions dishonorable and prejudicial to the welfare of the league and to the game of hockey.

Mulvey sued and later settled out of court.

QUINN AFFAIR

One of the most bizarre situations in NHL history involved the Kings and their coach Pat Quinn in the 1986-87 season. On December 22, 1986, the Kings played an early evening game in Calgary. At dinner after the game, the Kings' Marcel Dionne got a call from a Vancouver radio station asking him what he knew about Kings coach Pat Quinn agreeing to become the general manager of the Vancouver Canucks. Dionne knew nothing about it, which is unusual, because Marcel was usually up to date on the "scoops" around the league.

Later that night in the hotel, the door to my room was open as Quinn passed.

"Should I congratulate you now or later?" I asked.

Pat Quinn—Kings Coach, 1984-1987.
PHOTO BY ANDREW BERNSTEIN, COURTESY OF THE LOS ANGELES KINGS

He laughed it off but later made this statement to the media, "I have a moral and legal obligation to the Kings. I'm not going anywhere."

The following night, the Kings played in Vancouver and lost 6-4. Since it was the final game before the Christmas break, the team had a little party at the hotel. Quinn arrived at about 11:30 p.m., stayed only about 15 minutes, and left. I just thought he was upset about the loss and didn't feel in a party mood. It was later divulged that Quinn left to meet that night with Canucks officials, and according to a subsequent NHL report, he executed a written contact to become president and general manager of Vancouver. The Canucks were not a good team that year, finishing last in the Smythe Division and drawing small, quiet crowds.

On the Kings' bus to the airport the next morning, not knowing that Quinn had agreed to become an executive with Vancouver I said to him, "Pat, can you imagine watching shitty hockey like that every night?"

He nodded his head and mumbled something, and I didn't realize until weeks later the cutting nature of my remark.

On January 8, 1987, Kings owner Dr. Jerry Buss informed the NHL that Quinn had agreed to join Vancouver at the end of the current season. NHL president John Ziegler Jr. launched a full investigation into the matter, wherein he discovered that, in the Kings' contract with Quinn, the Kings had an option to extend Quinn's contract for one more year by giving Quinn notice to that effect prior to October 1, 1986.

In early December, Vancouver discovered that no "notice of employment" regarding Quinn had been filed with the NHL. Quinn's representative told Vancouver that Quinn was free to discuss employment with Vancouver. On December 9, Vancouver delivered to Quinn a written offer to become president and general manager of the Canucks beginning July 1, 1987. Quinn was to receive $100,000 USD as a signing bonus on or before January 23, 1987.

On December 26, 1986, Quinn told the Kings that he had taken a job with Vancouver but suggested it be kept confidential so he could finish the season as the Kings coach. Kings general manager Rogie Vachon informed Kings owner Dr. Jerry Buss of the situation later that day. Quinn continued to coach the Kings to victories over Boston and Philadelphia on December 27 and 30.

On January 2, 1987, the Kings were in Vancouver for a game that night; at the morning skate, Vancouver's check for $100,000 was delivered to Quinn. Quinn did not inform the Kings about the acceptance of the check.

On January 30, Ziegler handed down his decision. He said, "Although all parties believed they were doing that which was correct, legal, and proper, it is clear that at some point everyone forgot the essential and crucial element of the professional sports business, to wit, the integrity of the competition. By neglecting and failing to remove Quinn as coach from December 26, 1986, to January 9, 1987, Los Angeles permitted a serious threat to the integrity of each game."

He then fined the Kings $10,000 for each day Quinn was not removed as coach for a total of $130,000.

As for Vancouver, Ziegler said, "By its payment of $100,000 in midseason to a coach of a competing team, its closest competitor, it put in jeopardy every game that Quinn would coach for the remainder of the season. In addition, they should have known that, once they had reached their agreement, Quinn could no longer remain coach of Los Angeles. Consequently, for each of the days between December 11, 1986, the date of the agreement in principle and January 9, 1987, Vancouver is fined $10,000 per day for a total of $280,000. In addition for meeting with Quinn while he was still coach of Los Angeles, Vancouver is fined $20,000."

Pat Quinn got himself into some deep trouble by agreeing to a job with Vancouver while still coaching the Kings. *PHOTO COURTESY OF THE VANCOUVER CANUCKS*

For paying Quinn bonus money to sign, the Canucks were fined an additional $10,000. The total of fines levied on Vancouver was $310,000.

Ziegler also ordered the expulsion of Quinn from the NHL until the Kings and Canucks had completed their regular-season and playoff games. In addition, Quinn was suspended from performing any coaching duties for Vancouver at any time for three years prior to the start of training camp in 1990. Quinn was also suspended from performing any functions or attending league meetings or drafts. He could not conduct any transactions with any other teams, players, draft choices, coaches, assistant coaches, or scouts until after the conclusion of the 1987 annual meeting of the NHL Board of Governors.

One wondered how Quinn, who had a law degree, thought he could continue coaching the Kings while signed with Vancouver. He would have been privy to Kings' plans for players, trades, draft choices, and other affairs, all the while knowing he would be working for their closest competitor.

The Kings then announced that assistant coach Mike Murphy would be head coach for the remainder of the season and that negotiations were underway for a longer contract.

THE 'JAVELIN' INCIDENT

Early in the 1991-92 season, a bizarre incident took place in front of a sold-out crowd 16,005 during a Kings home game. Kings head coach Tom Webster had been bothered by an inner-ear problem that affected his balance. He missed three games with the condition on November 7, 9, and 11. He was back behind the bench on November 12 at Vancouver, but the Kings lost 8-2.

On November 16, the Detroit Red Wings were in Los Angeles, and the incident took place 6:21 into the second period. Kings defenseman Larry Robinson was given a two-minute penalty for cross-checking and a 10-minute penalty for game misconduct. Coach Webster was incensed by the call, so he picked up a hockey stick. As referee Kerry Fraser skated in the vicinity of the Kings bench, Webster, holding the stick javelin-style, let it fly at Fraser.

Luckily, the stick didn't strike the referee, but Webster was ejected from the game, and the Kings lost 5-3.

Webster coached four more games, but on November 27, NHL Executive Vice President Brian O'Neill suspended Webster for 12 games and the team was fined $10,000. The

Tom Webster–Kings Coach, 1989-1992. *PHOTO COURTESY OF THE LOS ANGELES KINGS*

suspension started on November 28 and lasted through December 29. Assistant coaches Cap Raeder and Rick Wilson handled the coaching duties. The Kings went 3-8-1 in that stretch.

Webster returned to coach on December 31 in Vancouver, and the Kings lost 5-3. Two nights later, Webster got his 100th career-coaching victory as the Kings beat Edmonton 5-3 in L.A.

The Kings probably never again used the term, "Let's stick it to 'em."

FOUR IS BETTER THAN THREE

On October 15, 1974, the Kings were the opponents in the first-ever NHL game played at home by the Washington Capitals. The Kings had opened the season with a win in Philadelphia, a tie at Montreal, and a win in Buffalo. The Capitals had entered the NHL that season and had opened with losses at New York against the Rangers and at Minnesota.

Kings owner Jack Kent Cooke was also part owner of the Washington Redskins of the National Football League, who were coached by George Allen. Allen was known as a master motivator, and Cooke decided it would be a good idea for Allen to give the Kings a pep talk prior to the game. This did not meet with overwhelming approval by Kings coach Bob Pulford, but he went along with it.

As the Kings left the hotel and boarded the team bus to leave for the game, Pulford and Allen stood at the bus door, and as each player filed on, Pulford introduced them to Allen. When everyone was seated, Allen stood up in front of the bus and, as was his habit, was licking his fingers and clapping his hands as he talked. He reminded the Kings, in his gravelly voice, that the home crowd would energize the Capitals, and that they would be highly motivated to win their first-ever NHL contest at home. He urged the Kings not to allow the Caps to score first and gain momentum. Aware that the Kings were unbeaten in three straight, Allen then said, "Remember men, four is better than three," and then he left the bus.

As the bus pulled away, there was silence. The Kings had a journeyman defenseman named Larry Brown who wore No. 3. Finally, one of the players shouted, "That shows how much he knows about hockey, he thinks Bobby Orr [who wore No. 4] is better than Larry Brown." The bus erupted in laughter.

The Kings did not heed Allen's warning as they let the Capitals score first, but the Kings came back to tie, and the game ended 1-1. Maybe Allen's pep talk did have an effect, since the Kings were unbeaten in 16 of their first 17 games that season, going 10-1-6.

DON'T COUNT CHICKENS

The old adage, "Don't count your chickens before they're hatched," came true for me in a most embarrassing way at the end of the 2003-04 season.

On March 16, 2004, Coach Andy Murray needed just one more victory—with 11 games remaining—to become the winningest coach in Kings history. The producer of our television-pregame show wanted me to interview Murray before the game that night with the St. Louis Blues. I figured the Kings would beat the Blues, so my final words of the interview were, "Andy, let me be the first to congratulate you on becoming the Kings' winningest coach ever."

Well, not only did the Kings lose that night, they went on to lose 11-straight games to finish the season, a club-record. After each loss, our television producer, Bob Borgen, would point at me on the bus or plane and say, "It's your fault." Never in the world did I think Andy wouldn't get that one victory before the end of the season.

The most bizarre and devastating loss came in the final game of the season at San Jose. The Kings had a 3-1 lead with just over 20 seconds remaining. On television, we had a shot of Murray on the bench, and I was seconds away from saying, "*Now*, Andy Murray will be the winningest coach in Kings history."

Fortunately, I didn't say that because what followed was the most unbelievable ending I've ever seen. The Sharks pulled their goaltender for an extra attacker, and defenseman Brad Stuart scored with 20 seconds left to pull San Jose within a goal at 3-2. Seventeen seconds later, Stuart scored again to tie the game and send it to overtime. Three minutes and ten seconds into overtime, Vincent Damphousse scored to give San Jose the 4-3 win and the Kings their 11th-consecutive loss to end the season.

I'd never seen Murray so despondent. He sat, slumped in his seat, and didn't say a single word on the flight home. When we landed, he bolted off the plane and was about 100 yards ahead of everyone as he walked to his car.

The following year, 2004-05, was the NHL lockout, canceling the season; so Murray didn't get another chance until the first game of the 2005-06 season in Dallas. The Kings jumped out to a 4-0 lead at the end of the first period. Again, it looked as if Murray would attain that elusive record-breaking win, but Dallas came back with five straight goals and won 5-4.

Finally, the next night—October 6, 2005—the Kings beat the Phoenix Coyotes 3-2 in front of a sold-out crowd of 18,118 in the home opener, and Andy Murray had win No. 179, passing Bob Pulford as the Kings' all-time winningest coach.

I'd learned my lesson, though—never predict while announcing sports.

THE COBRA

From 1976 to 1978, the Kings had a backup goaltender named Gary "Cobra" Simmons. The nickname came from the picture of a green cobra snake on the front of his black goalie mask. He didn't play very often, but on March 9, 1978, Cobra got the call to mind the net on the road against the Buffalo Sabres. It was his first start in 20 games—and he was a little rusty. The Sabres scored the first two goals.

"I was so slow on one of them I even missed it coming *out* of the net," Cobra said.

The Kings rallied, and the game ended 3-3. Afterward, a reporter asked Cobra, who had just played his first game in 48 days, if he thought he would start the next game.

"What do you think I am?" Cobra answered. "A f—ing machine?"

TRIPLE-CROWN LINE

On January 13, 1979, Kings head coach Bob Berry made a monumental decision. Hockey coaches are always tinkering with line combinations—whom to play together on the wings with a certain center, always looking for that chemistry that will make the line click. That night, with the Kings playing in Detroit, Berry decided to put left wing Charlie Simmer and

Charlie Simmer—Left Wing on the Triple-Crown Line.
PHOTO COURTESY OF THE LOS ANGELES KINGS

Hockey Hall of Famer Marcel Dionne—Center on the Triple-Crown Line.
PHOTO COURTESY OF THE LOS ANGELES KINGS

right wing Dave Taylor together with center Marcel Dionne. That was the start of one of the highest scoring lines in NHL history.

The Kings beat Detroit that night 7-3, and that line came to be known as the Triple-Crown Line. The next full season they were together, they compiled 328 points, the second most in one season of any line in league history. Dionne finished that season with 137 points and the NHL scoring title. Simmer shared the league lead with 56 goals and set a modern-day NHL record by scoring a goal in 13 consecutive games, and Taylor, despite missing 19 games with a knee injury, still managed to score 90 points. From January 13, 1979, to November 17, 1979, that line scored at least a point in 56 straight games.

Each player was a perfect complement for the others, and they had that sixth sense of where each would be on the ice at any given moment. Dave Taylor was the banger in the corners, and he would get control of the puck. Dionne was what they call a pure goal scorer—one who had that special knack for putting the puck in the net. Simmer, while also a great goal scorer, tallied most of his from close range of the net and was also adept at having the puck glance off his body for a score.

The most devastating night that line experienced was on March 2, 1981, at Maple Leaf Gardens in Toronto. Simmer had scored 56 goals in 65 games and was the team's leading goal scorer as the Kings met the Maple Leafs. At one point in the game, Simmer was chasing one of the Toronto players and went to turn to go after the puck. Toronto defenseman Borje Salming just nicked his shoulder, but spun him around. As Simmer put it, "I skated around my foot."

In other words, one foot stayed anchored while his body twisted around it and caused a spiral fracture of his right leg.

In the booth, I could tell it seemed to be a severe injury, but my first indication of how serious was when Marcel Dionne skated over to Simmer, took one look at his leg, and started shaking his head. In my earphone, our producer in the remote truck was telling me it was a broken leg. I wanted to know who was giving him that information and how accurate it was before I mentioned that on the air.

The trainers took Simmer into the Toronto dressing room because it was the closest to the area where the injury had occurred.

"What do you think?" the doctor asked Charlie.

"I broke my leg," Charlie replied.

"How do you know?" the doctor inquired.

"I broke my f—-ing leg!" he hollered back again.

Dave Taylor—Right Wing on the Triple-Crown Line; Kings General
Manager, 1997-2006. *PHOTO COURTESY OF THE LOS ANGELES KINGS*

They taped both of his legs together, and when the
ambulance attendants dropped the stretcher off the curb and
headed to the ambulance, Charlie said it started to hurt.

When they arrived at the hospital, shock started to set in. The
nurses said to Simmer, "We were watching the game on
television, and we knew you were coming here." Simmer had
surgery the next morning, and his season was finished.

Looking back on the injury, Simmer said, "If you're going to break your leg, you want to do it on a Saturday night with the game being televised coast to coast on *Hockey Night in Canada*. That way everyone can see it. You don't want to do it on a Thursday night in Pittsburgh."

Eight days later on March 10, 1981, the Kings traded their first-round choice in the 1983 draft and their third-round choice in the 1981 draft to the Buffalo Sabres for high-scoring winger Rick Martin to compensate for the offensive loss of Simmer. Martin had twice scored more than 50 goals a season. The trade turned out to be a disaster. Martin had a knee injury, but doctors in Buffalo and in Los Angeles assured Kings general manager George Maguire that Martin could play. One morning shortly after the trade, Maguire asked me to go to the L.A. airport and pick up Martin. As I waited at the curb, I could see Martin walking toward me almost dragging one leg. I introduced myself and told him I would drive him to the Forum. As he got in my car, he had to lift his leg with two hands just to bend his knee. I thought, "We traded a No.1 draft choice for this?"

As it turned out, Rick Martin played only four games for the Kings, scoring two goals and four assists for six points. One night, shortly thereafter prior to a game at the Forum, the Kings called a press conference to announce that Martin's knees were so bad he would have to retire. A reporter for KABC radio, the late Liz Shanov, asked the Kings' George Maguire if Scotty Bowman, then-general manager at Buffalo, had screwed him on the deal.

George replied, "Scotty Bowman couldn't screw anybody, including you."

By the way, with the No. 1 draft choice that Buffalo received from the Kings in the 1983 draft, the Sabres chose Tom Barrasso, who went on to become one of the most dominant goaltenders in the NHL.

DIONNE DEATH THREAT

Marcel Dionne played 12 years for the Kings and remains the team's all-time leading scorer. He was the first true superstar to wear a Kings uniform, and he was a favorite among Kings fans who marveled at this scoring ability; but apparently that appreciation was not shared in other arenas around the NHL.

On January 27, 1979, the Kings were playing in Pittsburgh, and Dionne received a phone call that afternoon at the team hotel. The caller said, "I have a high-powered rifle; and if you score a goal tonight, I'm going to blow your head off."

Dionne told Coach Bob Berry, who told him not to tell anyone else on the team, and then he reported the threat to security. Security told Dionne they thought it was a hoax, but he didn't have to play if he didn't feel safe. Marcel said he was going to play, and the NHL provided security for him as he entered and exited the ice. On the ice, however, he was on his own.

Dionne was not known to exert himself too much during the pregame warm-up. He would usually skate leisurely around the ice, but on that night during the warm-up he was skating fast and zigzagging all over the ice, feeling that it would be hard to hit a moving target. His teammates, not knowing the situation, wondered what had gotten into Marcel. During the national anthem, Marcel felt he was a "sitting duck" on the bench, so he kept rocking from side to side.

When the game started, linemates Dave Taylor and Charlie Simmer kept passing the puck to Dionne, but Marcel wanted no part of it so he kept passing it back. He even passed up a couple of great scoring opportunities, thinking he would be shot if he scored. Finally, he had the puck with a wide-open net and couldn't do anything but score.

After the puck went in, Marcel said, "I looked for the biggest guys on the ice and skated into the middle of them trying to hide."

Marcel Dionne, Kings all-time leading scorer with 1,307 points.

Dionne scored two goals that night, the Kings won 5-3, and fortunately, the call was a hoax.

The next day, word of the death threat got out; and the next time the Kings played in Pittsburgh, security screened all the team's phone calls. Marcel said he had put the threat out of his mind, but his teammates apparently thought the person who made the threat might be in the crowd. In hockey, the custom is, when a player scores a goal, his teammates on the ice skate over to congratulate him. That night, when Marcel scored, all of his teammates scattered in all different directions, just in case. Charlie Simmer said, "When a teammate scores a goal. and you return to the bench, you want to sit close to him because you know the television cameras will be focused on him. But not that night—we all gave Marcel plenty of room on the bench."

Marcel said when he tells that story now at various functions, he says, "We never played as a team because nobody wanted to die as a team."

CAN YOU SAY THAT ON TV?

One never knows how players are going to react or what they will say on live television.

Dave "Tiger" Williams played for the Kings from 1984 to 1988 appearing in 162 games scoring 40 goals and 50 assists for 90 points, but he was best known for his volatile play on the ice and for amassing 962 penalty minutes in a Kings uniform. That total pales in comparison to his final career total of 3,966 penalty minutes, which is a NHL record. On describing himself as a player he responded, "Never surrender—I wanted everybody to be like me. If they didn't put their life on the line, I wouldn't like them, their wife, or their family."

Tiger was known for saying things without regard to the consequences. One time, while boarding a commercial flight in

Dave "Tiger" Williams—Kings Left Wing, 1984-1988.
PHOTO COURTESY OF THE LOS ANGELES KINGS

Los Angeles, Tiger spotted a passenger we didn't know smoking a cigarette in *Tiger's* seat. Tiger pounced. "You stupid bastard, don't you know you're not supposed to smoke while the plane is at the gate?" The startled passenger quickly extinguished his cigarette. Another time on a commercial flight, Tiger was putting his luggage in the overhead bin when he spotted a woman coming down the aisle wearing the ugliest hat of all time. As she passed Tiger, he said, "Lady, don't tell me you paid for that hat."

On December 5, 1985, the Kings were playing in Edmonton and were losing 4-0 early in the second period. They then scored four straight on goals by Dave Taylor, Brian MacLellan, Garry Galley, and Phil Sykes to tie the score. In the third period, Williams scored with 2:58 left in the game and the Kings led 6-5. However, with 41 seconds remaining, the Oilers tied the score, and the game ended 6-6 in overtime.

On a live postgame TV interview, my partner Nick Nickson said to Williams, "Tiger, I thought you had scored the game winning goal."

Tiger responded, "Mr. Nickson, it should have been the game-winning goal, but each time this team gets close to winning we just …" and with this Tiger grabbed his throat with both hands and started choking himself, "… aaarrrggghhh."

Nickson then mentioned that the Oilers had outshot the Kings 46 to 26 in the game, and Tiger said, "Yes, but a lot of those were wimp-ass shots."

We didn't do too many more live interviews with Tiger.

***

Another incident involving Tiger Williams occurred at the Kings practice facility, the Culver City Ice Rink. The Kings dressing room was located upstairs on the second floor and was a long and narrow room. The players' lockers were across from each other so that when they were sitting and bent over tying their skates, there wasn't much more than a narrow pathway down the middle. As the players arrived for practice this particular day, Bernie Nicholls noticed two boxes filled with copies of a new book written by Tiger Williams. The books had been delivered to Tiger at the practice rink. Tiger had not arrived in the room so, as a joke, Nicholls passed out the book saying they were a gift from Tiger. Tiger had no intention of "giving" the books away; he was going to sell them.

Tiger had been in the medical room talking with trainer Pete Demers and a friend who was showing him a high-tech bow and arrow. Tiger was known for hunting bear with bow and arrow in the off-season. When Tiger got to the locker room, some of the players, including Nicholls, were mockingly thanking him for the gift. Tiger was so incensed he took the bow and arrow, hollered at Nicholls, and fired an arrow about eight inches into a metal air duct at the end of the room. If one player had leaned the wrong way, or someone had gotten up and walked into the middle of the room at the instant Tiger fired, the outcome would have been disastrous.

***

Another player's reaction on a live postgame interview took us by surprise. It was on January 21, 1985, again in Edmonton. The Kings led 4-0 in the first period on goals by Brian MacLellan, Bob Miller (not me), Marcel Dionne, and Carl Mokosak. Dionne's goal was the 611th of his career to move him past Bobby Hull into third place all time on the NHL goal-scoring list. By the end of the second period, the Kings led 7-3 and were well on their way to a victory over a strong Edmonton team, or so we thought. The Oilers scored five goals in the third period to win 8-7.

Nickson's live guest on the TV postgame show that night was Kings right-winger Jim Fox. Fox was so distraught and upset over the way the Kings blew the game that he was actually in tears. When Nick asked what went wrong he said, "Who cares? It happened. … We're awful." Fox later said he was frustrated and at a loss for words, and he felt ashamed that he actually cried on live television. I told him I thought it was one of the greatest reactions I had ever seen because it showed everyone his true emotions and the true competitive nature of the sport, i.e., how much they want to win.

I thought it was a great moment of live television.

RANDY HOLT

Usually, you never have players react to comments you make on the air, but once in a while, a player or his wife will take exception to something they think they heard. Most often it's something heard second-hand, and often the wrong person gets blamed.

On January 19, 1980, the Kings were playing the Atlanta Flames at the Forum in Los Angeles when a sickening incident occurred. At 6:56 of the second period, Bob MacMillan of Atlanta was called for high sticking, but as he skated to center ice, Randy Holt of the Kings came up behind him and struck him in the right eye with the blade of his stick. MacMillan went down, and the crowd fell silent as most of them thought, me included, that he had suffered a serious eye injury.

Holt was given a five-minute major penalty for intent to injure and a 10-minute major for match misconduct. Both of those penalties require a referee's report to the league for possible further disciplinary action. As Holt skated off the ice, the *home* crowd lustily booed him for such a cowardly act.

Holt played only 78 games for the Kings over two years, 1978-79 and 1979-80. He scored no goals, had seven assists, and a whooping 296 penalty minutes, so you know what his skill level was and what role he played on the team.

After the game, Kings general manager George Maguire said to me, "Randy Holt wants to see you in my office and bring your tape recorder."

In Maguire's office, Holt looked at me and said, "Do you consider yourself part of this team?"

"Yes."

"Then why would you say on the air that I should be banned from the NHL for life?"

"I didn't say that."

"My wife told me that's what you said."

Maguire told me to replay the tape recording of my play-by-play of the incident. I did, and, of course, nothing was on the tape because I didn't say anything of the sort. Maguire then told Holt to get out of his office.

I then said to Maguire, "Don't ever ask me to come in here again and justify to a player what I say on the air."

I later found out it was the Atlanta announcer, Jiggs McDonald, who was so upset by Holt's actions that he said he should be banned for life.

Fortunately, MacMillan was all right, and his career was not shortened by the injury.

FOXED OUT OF A GOAL

On the Kings' all-time scoring list, my broadcast partner, Jim Fox, is credited with 186 goals in his NHL career, but it should be 187.

On February 1, 1987, the Kings were playing the Quebec Nordiques in Quebec City when Fox ripped a shot into the net. The puck went in, hit the metal bar in the back of the net, and came out so fast that play continued as the Nordiques headed down the ice with the puck. Fox, meanwhile, stayed in front of

Jim Fox–Kings Right Wing, 1980-1990; Kings Color Commentator, 1990-present. *PHOTO COURTESY OF THE LOS ANGELES KINGS*

the Quebec net, slamming his stick on the ice, jumping up and down, and screaming that he had scored. He didn't attempt to join the play at the other end. On our telecast, I said that Fox had scored, but then I had my doubts as play continued. At a break in the action, we showed a replay, and sure enough, the puck went right into the middle of the net. In those days, there was no television replay for officials to check.

By coincidence, the referee in that game, Andy Van Hellemond, had asked the Kings before the game if he could ride on their charter flight to Toronto that night. The Kings agreed. On the bus to the airport, Van Hellemond was sitting in an aisle seat next to me when Fox boarded, stopped in the aisle, and stared at Van Hellemond. The referee said, "Jim, I'm sorry, I didn't see it go in the net, nor did either of the linesmen. I can't call a goal if I didn't see it."

Van Hellemond told me the officials looked at a television replay between periods and knew the goal should have counted. He also said to the linesmen, "Watch, this will end up a one-goal game."

Sure enough, it ended Quebec 3 - Kings 2.

KELLY VERSUS HOWE

Gordie Howe had a remarkable career in hockey playing for 26 seasons in the NHL, 25 of those with the Detroit Red Wings and one with the Hartford Whalers. In addition, he played six seasons in the World Hockey Association, playing with two of his sons. He retired when he was 52 years old after playing 2,186 total games.

On December 12, 1979, Howe had a rude awakening while playing for the Whalers against the Kings in Los Angeles. Unfortunately, only 8,732 fans were on hand to see one of the greatest players in the history of the game, although he was at the end of his career.

The Kings had a muscular young rookie named John Paul Kelly, and he made a name for himself on that night. As Howe brought the puck to center ice, Kelly threw a body check and knocked Howe completely over the boards into the penalty box.

The crowd gasped as they saw Howe tumble out of sight. Kelly said later, "I thought, 'Oh, my God … I've checked a 52-year-old grandfather, the legendary Gordie Howe, over the boards.'"

Howe said later he thought there was Plexiglas in front of the penalty box, and he would just take the check and bounce off the glass, but there was no glass at that point.

Howe was known throughout his career for having the "sharpest elbows in hockey" and he wasn't shy about using them to inflict bodily harm on opponents. Players on the bench told coach Bob Berry that he'd better get J.P. off the ice before Howe went at him. Nothing further occurred between Howe and Kelly, but it was a sight to remember.

VACHON GOAL

On February 15, 1977, hockey fans at the L.A. Forum thought they had been in on hockey history. This was the 59th year of the NHL and the 14,280th game; up to that time, no goalie had ever been credited with scoring a goal.

With the Kings leading the New York Islanders 1-0 in the first period, a delayed penalty was called against the Kings' Bert Wilson. The Islanders, in possession of the puck, pulled goalie Glenn "Chico" Resch for an extra attacker, and teammate Bryan Trottier passed the puck from deep in the Kings' zone to his defensemen at the Kings' blue line. The puck went between the defensemen, however, and slid 188 feet into an empty net for a Kings goal.

The official scorer thought that Kings goalie Rogie Vachon had been the last King to touch the puck before the Islanders gained possession and that he should get credit for the goal. The 10,256 fans in attendance roared when Vachon's name was announced as the goal scorer. After the period, while listening to an audio tape of my play-by-play, I realized that, after Vachon had made a save, I had said that the Kings' Vic Venasky played the puck, so it couldn't have been Vachon's goal. I mentioned this to the scorer, and after some discussion, the goal was changed to Venasky.

Sorry Rogie!

Vachon did get the shutout in a 3-0 win.

For your information, Billy Smith, who was the Islanders' backup goalie that night, became the first goalie to get credit for a goal on November 28, 1979, against the Colorado Rockies.

ISAKSSON

In the 1982-83 season the Kings had a player from Sweden named Ulf Isaksson. He only played one year in the NHL and was better known for sleeping than for playing. The Kings players called him a *mattress back*.

On January 16, 1983, against the Devils in New Jersey, it was obvious to Ulf that he was not going to see much ice time, so he sat at one end of the bench with his skates untied, his gloves off, and a towel around neck. He was just relaxing, watching the game.

In the second period, Brian MacLellan of the Kings received a two-minute minor penalty for roughing and a five-minute major for fighting. Someone had to serve the minor penalty and coach Don Perry decided it would be Isaksson. Perry hollered Ulf's name, and Ulf thought he was going to play; so he hastily tied his skates, put on his gloves, got rid of the towel, jumped over the boards, and was ready for the face-off. The referee, however, promptly told Ulf to go to the penalty box. Perplexed, Ulf thought *he* was penalized, and without a good command of English kept telling the referee, "I did nosing ... I did nosing."

He was finally convinced that indeed he did "nothing" and was just serving MacLellan's minor penalty.

ESA "PENIS"

One of the biggest changes and challenges over the past several years has been the influx of European players in the NHL and the effort it takes to pronounce their names correctly. In the 2003-04 season the Kings had a newcomer to the team, a forward from Finland named Esa Pirnes, pronounced PEER-nes. The potential for trouble concerning his last name never entered my mind, but disaster struck as the Kings were playing the Phoenix Coyotes one night at Staples Center.

The battle for the puck was along the boards when, on the air, I said, "Here is Esa Peni ... er, Pirnes." I didn't quite say the "s" in penis, but it sounded like it. I paused and then heard my partner Jim Fox on the talkback to the control room shouting, "Did he say it? Did he say it?" I couldn't speak for a few seconds, and the next time I looked toward Jim, his chair was empty. He was in the back of the booth, laughing so hard he was crying.

After the game, Kings coach Andy Murray played a tape of that incident for the entire team. The next morning, we were leaving on a road trip, and as I was walking toward the plane, Pirnes was walking toward me shaking his head. He told me that when he returned home that game, he had four messages on his voicemail from friends in Finland, saying, "Did that guy call you 'Penis?'"

We both had a good laugh and so did Esa's teammates. I told most other announcers in the NHL what had happened hoping I wouldn't be the only one to make that mistake. The next telecast, the first time Pirnes touched the puck, I said, "Here comes Esa Peeeer-nes to center ice." I still had to pause a bit before saying his name to make sure I enunciated correctly.

FINAL INTERMISSION

GRETZKY TO L.A.

Bruce McNall purchased 100 percent of the Kings team from Jerry Buss on March 23, 1988, and the rotund, jovial new owner made an immediate impact.

In the summer of 1988, there were rumors that the Kings were trying to acquire the greatest player in the game, Wayne Gretzky of the Edmonton Oilers. I thought it was too good to be true, but I wanted to find out for myself if the rumors had any validity. I phoned McNall under the pretense of talking about the television schedule for the coming season, and toward the end of the conversation, I went for it, saying, "When are you going to sign Gretzky?"

There was a lengthy pause and then Bruce said, "Tell me what you think of this: we unveil new silver-and-black uniforms, and Wayne Gretzky is our model."

I said it would be fantastic, so I knew a deal was in the works.

In early August, I was at the Forum when Jerry West, general manager of the Los Angeles Lakers, whispered to me, "The deal

Wayne Gretzky addresses media on the day he was traded to the Kings.
PHOTO BY ANDREW BERNSTEIN, COURTESY OF THE LOS ANGELES KINGS

is done." He said he had played golf with someone who told him that Gretzky was coming to the Kings.

Sure enough, the next day I got a call to be the master of ceremonies at the press conference that night at a Los Angeles hotel. The media response was unbelievable, with about 12 television stations, some going live on the air, and about 30 still photographers. At the dais, McNall made some introductions then said, with tongue in cheek, "… But now, the reason we're here, and the moment you've been waiting for, the introduction of our new team colors and uniforms."

He then paused for reaction then continued, "May we have our model please?"

Out stepped Wayne and Janet Gretzky. When Wayne put on his Kings jersey, the sound of the still cameras clicking was like machine-gun fire. As Gretzky was facing the audience, someone yelled in jest, "What number did you get?" as if he would get anything other than his famous No. 99

This was the biggest trade in sports history. At no other time had an athlete in his prime, one who dominated his sport the way Wayne Gretzky did, been traded.

Many people said it was like Babe Ruth being traded, but I disagree. When Ruth was traded from Boston to the New York Yankees, he wasn't the Ruth who later in his career dominated the game. This trade was headlines around the world. I had a friend who told me he was vacationing in Germany, and it made headlines in the papers there.

The reaction in Los Angeles was immediate. The Kings rose from near obscurity to one of the highest-profile teams in the United States and Canada. *Playboy* magazine called Gretzky, "Jim Thorpe on skates, Jesse Owens with a stick, and Babe Ruth in hockey pants. On statistics alone, Gretzky is the greatest athlete of the 20th Century."

The Kings had to get extra help to man the phones in the ticket office to serve thousands calling to purchase season tickets. When told they weren't sure of the price of tickets, fans often said, "Here's my credit card, just fill it in later." The Kings sold something like 4,000 season tickets in a week, and their season-ticket base rose from 5,000 to 9,000. Kings merchandise—jersey, jackets, and caps—went from last in the NHL to the No. 1-selling item and were in great demand throughout the U.S. and Canada, not just in L.A. In fact, while on vacation in Europe, I saw someone wearing a Kings T-shirt in Rothenburg, Germany, and a street sweeper wearing a Kings hat in Salzburg, Austria. The trade also had an impact on the Kings television schedule, which was increased from 37 to 62 games.

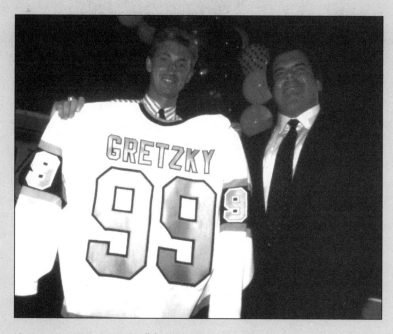

Kings owner Bruce McNall brought Wayne Gretzky to the Kings in 1988.
PHOTO BY ANDREW BERNSTEIN, COURTESY OF THE LOS ANGELES KINGS

Reaction around the NHL included Emile Francis, general manager of the Hartford Whalers saying, "The Kings went from the outhouse to the penthouse in one fell swoop." The Kings were now the "in" team in Hollywood. McNall had a "Meet the Kings" party at famous Chasen's restaurant in Beverly Hills. In attendance were Milton Berle, Michael J. Fox, John Candy, Neil Diamond, Mary Hart, Alan Thicke, and Jamie Farr. Season-ticket holders included Magic Johnson, Rob Lowe, and Tom Hanks. Former president Ronald Reagan and wife, Nancy, watched many games from ice level at the glass.

Some loyal Kings fans had a different reaction however. Gretzky was not a favorite of Kings fans when he played for

Edmonton. One night in a game at the Forum, the Kings' Dave Taylor took a swing at Gretzky and just grazed him, but Gretzky fell to the ice as if he'd been shot. Wayne was peeking up at the referee to see if a penalty was being called. It was, and then Gretzky jumped up and continued playing as the crowd lustily booed. Kings fans would wave white handkerchiefs at Gretzky because he was always "crying" over missed calls by the referee. When Gretzky came to the Kings, those same fans came to games wearing buttons that read, "I was a Kings fan BG," *Before Gretzky*. They almost seemed to resent the fact that so many new fans jumped on the Kings bandwagon.

The first game for Wayne in a Kings uniform was October 6, 1988, and a sellout crowd packed the building and roared their approval as Gretzky was introduced. In typical Gretzky fashion, he scored on his first shot on goal at 12:54 of the first period and finished with a goal and three assists in a 8-2 Kings win over Detroit.

I have told people that those of us who were able to see Wayne Gretzky night after night were fortunate. I always approached our telecast each night as if I might see and be able to describe something that I'd never seen before. I feel, years from now, fans are going to ask us what it was like watching him play in person, much as you would ask someone who saw Babe Ruth in his prime.

5

OVERTIME

GRETZKY RECORDS

October 15, 1989, will go down in National Hockey League history as a most significant date. That's the night Wayne Gretzky became the greatest scorer in the history of the game. He passed the legendary Gordie Howe with his 1,851st point, and he did it in true Gretzky fashion.

First let's go back to the summer of 1989. It was obvious that Gretzky would break Howe's record early in the coming season. One day, a friend of mine asked me what I was going to say when it happened. I told him I was just going to do the play-by-play and hope I didn't make a mistake because I would hear it the rest of my life. But then, he said, "Aren't you going to say something special?"

I hadn't thought about that, but then I thought people apparently expect something more than just the description of the play. I started jotting down some ideas, but I didn't want it to sound rehearsed. The night of the game, I told our television

"The Great One," Wayne Gretzky. *PHOTO COURTESY OF THE LOS ANGELES KINGS*

producer, Mark Stulberger, to give me about six seconds to say something after it happened; and then I would be quiet, and he could get crowd noise and reaction shots.

The moment came, of all places, in Edmonton, where Gretzky had so many great moments playing for the Oilers. At the start of the game, I asked my partner, Nick Nickson, to help me out and point to the ice when Gretzky was playing and away from the ice when he was on the bench. That may sound stupid, but I didn't want Gretzky to jump on the ice, "on the fly," when I'd be unaware of his presence. As it turned out, fans watching on television and listening on radio appreciated that since, when I said Gretzky is on the ice, they would be on the edge of their chairs; and when I said he was on the bench, they would relax. They didn't know I was doing it more for myself than for their benefit.

Wayne Gretzky with the puck from his 802nd goal, which made him the greatest goal-scorer in NHL history. From left: Luc Robitaille, Bob Miller, Gretzky, and Marty McSorley. *PHOTO BY ART FOXALL, COURTESY OF THE LOS ANGELES KINGS*

Wayne Gretzky with the puck from his 802nd goal, which made him the greatest goal-scorer in NHL history.
PHOTO BY ART FOXALL, COURTESY OF THE LOS ANGELES KINGS

The historic moment came with just 53 seconds remaining in regulation. The Oilers, leading 4-3, won a face-off in their zone. Oilers defenseman Kevin Lowe cleared the puck high in the air, but Kings defenseman Steve Duchesne knocked it down at the blue line and passed to Dave Taylor, who slid the puck to his left to Gretzky—who then backhanded it past Oilers goalie Bill Ranford. As the Kings players streamed onto the ice, I said, "Wayne Gretzky, the Great One, has become the greatest of them all—the leading scorer in the history of the National Hockey League."

Nothing profound, but at least it put a capper on the moment.

Some events in Gretzky's career seem to be right out of a Hollywood script, and this was one of those moments. Play was stopped for an on-ice ceremony featuring Gordie Howe; Wayne; his wife, Janet; his father, Walter; Kings owner Bruce McNall; Scotty Morrison from the Hockey Hall of Fame; and NHL President John Ziegler, Jr. In his remarks Gretzky said, "Maybe it is only fitting that a reward such as this takes a lot of teamwork and a lot of help; and both teams here today are definitely a big part of the 1,800 points I've gotten in my career."

There was still a game to finish, and it went into overtime, where the Kings won 5-4 on a wrap-around goal by—you guessed it—Wayne Gretzky.

To give you an idea of how great Gretzky was, it took Howe 26 seasons to reach 1,850 points, and Gretzky broke the record just six games into his 12th season. Four seasons later, Gretzky was set to break another of Howe's records, the one for *goals* scored in the NHL. This time it came in front of a home crowd at the Forum on March 23, 1994. The sell-out crowd of 16,005 anticipated this would be the night that they'd witness hockey history. There were over 100 requests for press credentials for that game. Again I thought, "I've got to come up with something special to say after he scores."

The historic moment came at 14:47 of the second period against the Vancouver Canucks. Luc Robitaille passed to Gretzky, who then passed to Marty McSorley on the right side. As Vancouver goalie Kirk McLean came out to play a possible shot by McSorley, Marty slid the puck across the ice to his left to Gretzky, who was wide open, along with the net. As he scored, I said on television, "Wayne Gretzky's NHL record book

Wayne Gretzky addresses the crowd after scoring his 802nd goal. PHOTO COURTESY OF THE LOS ANGELES KINGS

is now complete. He's the all-time leader in points, assists, and now, with his 802nd goal, the all-time leading goal scorer in the history of the National Hockey League."

Gretzky broke the record in 650 games fewer than Howe took to reach 801.

Again, the game was stopped for an on-ice ceremony, which included Wayne's wife, Janet; his mother and father, Phyllis and Walter; and NHL Commissioner Gary Bettman. In Wayne's speech, he said, "To the fans of L.A., I've loved playing here for six years, and I hope I get another six years."

But that was not to happen.

GRETZKY TO ST. LOUIS

After eight years with the Kings, the unbelievable happened: the Kings traded Gretzky to St. Louis on February 27, 1996, for Craig Johnson, Patrice Tardif, Roman Vopat, and first- and fifth-round draft choices.

In January of that season, Gretzky delivered what some termed "an ultimatum" to the Kings: "Get some talent through immediate trades or trade me. I need to see action now. This city deserves to be winners. I'd like to win, and I'd like to see that happen."

He felt the Kings were two players away from contending for a Stanley Cup, and he was frustrated over management's inability to pull off a trade. He wanted them to acquire a 50-goal scorer and an offensive-minded defenseman. Gretzky would have become an unrestricted free agent that coming summer. In that situation, he would have been free to sign with any other team without the Kings receiving any compensation. "For me," said Gretzky, "I would like to have the opportunity to win a championship."

Gretzky's agent, Michael Barnett, held a meeting with Kings management on January 16 and said, "Ideally, a resolution will see him retire as a King and end all the rumors. No demand for a trade to another team was discussed today. It's not even in Wayne's thoughts at this time."

Sam McMaster, the Kings general manager, said of the meeting that day, "We discussed many things, including a contract extension for Wayne. Our goal is to build a winner and keep Wayne Gretzky as part of that organization."

On February 27, McMaster said the Kings offered Gretzky a two-year contract extension. On television that night, Gretzky told KCAL-TV that, as a result of that afternoon's meeting, the Kings left the decision to him, saying, "Do you want to sign with us, or do you want us to trade you?"

Gretzky went home, discussed the situation with his wife; and in a news conference at 8 p.m., the Kings announced they had traded Gretzky to St. Louis. Bob Sanderman, representing Kings owner Philip Anschutz and Ed Roski Jr., said, "Wayne let us know this afternoon that he preferred not to remain a Los Angeles King during his remaining active [playing] days." The Kings said they had also offered Wayne a "senior" position with the club when his playing days were over. They said he was the one who chose to leave.

Regardless, the Kings were roundly criticized in the media. Helene Elliott, of the *Los Angeles Times*, wrote, "Goodbye to the best player to ever wear a Kings uniform—or any other in hockey—and goodbye to all hopes of seeing the Kings rise above the mediocrity they have so tightly embraced for so many years."

Michael Ventre, in the *L.A. Daily News* was more blunt, "Trading Wayne Gretzky to the St. Louis Blues ranks as the all-time imbecilic act in the history of the Kings franchise."

So, the most exciting era in Kings hockey had ended.

During Gretzky's stay in L.A., there were reports—which he denied—that he had a hand in trades made by the team. This feeling was perpetuated, in my opinion, when on team flights after games, Wayne would sit next to owner McNall. I'm sure some players who may have struggled in the game that night felt that Wayne was telling Bruce they should be traded. Wayne admitted that there were times when the Kings were contemplating a trade and they would ask his opinion of certain players whom they might acquire, especially if he had played with those players. Certainly, that was a prudent thing to do—ask the opinion of as great a player as Gretzky. Another problem was, at times, McNall would invite several players to fly with him on his private jet to the next game rather than take the team plane. Those players included many of Gretzky's former Oilers teammates who were current members of the Kings; and there seemed to be some resentment among other players who called the exclusive group, "The Magnificent Seven."

6

PLAYOFFS

MIRACLE ON MANCHESTER

The greatest single game I have ever witnessed or been a part of was a 1982 playoff game between the Kings and the Edmonton Oilers. It's known as the "Miracle on Manchester," named for the street that runs by the Forum— then the Home of the Kings.

The best-of-five playoff series started in Edmonton, and the Oilers were heavily favored since they had finished the regular season with 111 points, second overall in the NHL. The Kings finished with 63 points, 17th overall. That was the lowest Kings point total in 10 years. The Oilers also boasted of a potent lineup that included Wayne Gretzky, who had scored a NHL-record 92 goals that season, Paul Coffey, Mark Messier, Jari Kurri, Kevin Lowe, and Grant Fuhr.

The first game of the series was played in Edmonton on April 7, 1982, and no one gave the Kings any chance for an upset. Playoff games are usually tight-checking, low-scoring affairs; but this night the Kings and Oilers set a NHL record for most goals by both teams with a total of 18 as the Kings won 10-8. The Oilers led 4-1 in the first period, but the Kings came back and led 8-6 at the end of the second. With the game tied 8-8 in the third period, Charlie Simmer scored as the puck bounced off his leg for a 9-8 Kings lead. Kings goalie Mario Lessard then stopped Gretzky on a breakaway, and Bernie Nicholls scored for the Kings into an empty net for the 10-8 victory.

The Oilers of that season were extremely arrogant, and that arrogance extended throughout the entire organization. They had a scout named Bob Freeman who sat in the booth right next to our broadcast location. The walls of the booth did not extend all the way out, so a person sitting in the next booth could hear what we were saying. At one point in the game, Gretzky was complaining to the referees about a call, and I said on the air, "Well, Wayne Gretzky is crying again to the officials."

Freeman overheard this and yelled at me, "Why don't you shut up? You don't know what you're talking about!" So when Nicholls scored into the empty net to secure the win, I really went overboard in my call of the goal just to irk Freeman. Nicholls had a celebration he did after scoring a goal that consisted of skating bent over, and pumping his arms back and forth. It became known as the "Pumpernicholl." When he scored into the empty net, I shouted, in an uncharacteristic display of *homerism*, "Do the 'Pumpernicholl,' Bernie. Yeah!"

The Oilers won the next game 3-2 in overtime on a goal by Gretzky, and the teams headed for Los Angeles with the series tied one game apiece. The scene was set for "The Miracle on Manchester."

It was April 10, 1982, and a full house of 16,005 filled the Forum in great anticipation of the Kings upsetting the Oilers. Their hopes were quickly dashed. Edmonton jumped out to a 5-0 lead at the end of two periods, and Gretzky was really putting on a show with two goals and two assists. The crowd

Bernie Nicholls, doing the "Pumpernicholl", holds the Kings record for goals in a single season—70 in 1988-89. PHOTO COURTESY OF THE LOS ANGELES KINGS

turned on Gretzky vocally, shouting obscenities at him—they booed him, and they waved white handkerchiefs at him because of his complaining about every referee's call that went against the Oilers. Oilers coach Glen Sather, who always had a smug smirk on his face, said of the Kings crowd, "The people here have the least amount of class in North America." Gretzky said the crowd didn't bother him.

The Oilers were completely outplaying and embarrassing the Kings. In fact, the Oilers were so arrogant that they were actually laughing at the Kings during play. I was so upset because I thought, "We do this every time: get everyone in L.A. excited about hockey and the Kings and then go right in the dumper." No one was prepared, however, for what would occur in the third period.

At 2:46 into that final period, Kings defenseman Jay Wells scored form the left point, and I thought, "At least we weren't going to get shut out." About three minutes later, Kings rookie Doug Smith, standing right in front of the net, put a shot up under the crossbar, and it was 5-2. The next goal didn't come until 5:22 remaining, when Charlie Simmer came from behind the net and jammed the puck past the right goal post to make it 5-3. At that point, the crowd was going crazy, and you could sense a feeling that maybe, just maybe, the Kings could come all the way back.

Kings owner Dr. Jerry Buss sat in a specially constructed private box, which consisted of four seats, at ice level right between the two benches. I noticed the box was empty, and I wondered on the air if the owner had left the game. I found out later Buss had a date with Kathy Crosby, and they had left to head for Palm Springs in a limousine. As the story goes, as they were listening to the game, the chauffeur turned and asked, "Should we go back?" to which Buss said, "No, it seems the farther away we get, the better they play." So the Kings owner missed the greatest comeback in Kings history.

Kings left wing Daryl Evans celebrates after scoring the game-winning, overtime goal in the "Miracle on Manchester." *PHOTO COURTESY OF THE LOS ANGELES KINGS*

With the Kings trailing 5-3, defenseman Mark Hardy scored on a weak shot from the top of the slot, which fooled Oilers goalie Grant Fuhr. With 4:01 left, it was 5-4. Now there was bedlam in the Forum. With 5:00 left, the Oilers Garry Unger had taken a five-minute major penalty for high sticking and cutting the Kings captain, Dave Lewis, on his eyebrow. Lewis got a two-minute minor for hooking, so the Kings eventually had a three-minute major power play. Still, the Oilers had chances to sew up the game. With 1:37 left, Kings goalie Mario Lessard stopped Edmonton's Pat Hughes on a breakaway. Then with 10 seconds left and the puck in the Oilers zone, Kings right wing Jim Fox made a great play—one that gave the Kings a chance. Gretzky had the puck on his stick, and all he had to do was clear it to center ice so time would run out. Fox, however, skated in front of Gretzky, took the puck away, and passed it to Hardy, who shot from the top of the slot. Fuhr made the save, but the rebound went right in front of the net to Kings rookie Steve Bozek, who scored to tie the game at 5-5.

When I looked at the scoreboard clock, it read 0:05 left.

During the wild finish, Lewis was getting stitched up in the Kings locker room. He said that, when Bozek scored, the doctor, in mid-stitch with needle in hand, pumped his arms in the air, scaring the hell out of Lewis. Meanwhile, in the arena, the crowd was frenzied, screaming, jumping up and down, and roaring. Yet they had 15 minutes to wait for the sudden-death overtime to start.

About a minute into overtime, my heart, and the hearts of 16,000 fans, sank as Lessard came sliding out of the Kings goal, giving Mark Messier a wide-open net. However, Messier shot it wide on his backhand. The Kings were still alive. Two-and-a-half minutes into overtime, there was a face-off in the Oilers zone to the left of goalie Grant Fuhr. The Kings had three rookies out on the forward line: Bozek, Smith, and Daryl Evans. Smith won the draw to Evans, who was positioned on right wing along the boards. Evans shot a one-timer right off the pass—a laser of a shot that went into the net over Fuhr's right shoulder.

The crowd erupted. Evans pirouetted the full length of the ice, twisting and turning, his stick in the air as his teammates leaped off the bench to chase him down and pile on him at the opposite end. The Kings had completed the greatest single-game comeback in NHL Stanley Cup playoff history with a 6-5 win.

Outside the Forum, a wild celebration was taking place in the parking lot. Fans were honking car horns and forming

Dave Lewis played a huge role in the "Miracle on Manchester."
PHOTO COURTESY OF THE LOS ANGELES KINGS

impromptu motorcades in the streets. Some had taken Oilers jerseys, tied them to their car bumpers, and were dragging them along. However, the series wasn't over yet. The Oilers won the next game in L.A. 3-2, and with the series tied two games apiece, the teams head back to Edmonton for the deciding game the *next* night.

After the Kings win in the "miracle" game, Scott Carmichael, the Kings public relations director, had been cheering in the hallway near the dressing rooms. When the Oilers won the next game, Edmonton coach Glen Sather said to Carmichael, "You aren't cheering tonight, are you?" and then swore at him. A

The "Fabulous" Forum–Home of the Los Angeles Kings from 1967 to 1999.
PHOTO BY WEN ROBERTS PHOTOGRAPHY INK

minor altercation ensued with Sather taking a swing and grabbing Carmichael's tie. Then some of the Oilers players intervened on behalf of Sather. A local sports reporter, Joe McDonnell, who was extremely heavy, then grabbed Sather from behind. Sather later said he got bear-hugged by a guy who outweighed him by 600 pounds.

Since only one charter plane could be found, both teams flew to Edmonton on the same plane, which was extremely rare. I had never heard of it happening before, and an insurance waiver had to be obtained. The Oilers boarded first and sat in the back, and the Kings sat in front. By the time the plane took off from

L.A., it was already 1:30 in the morning in Edmonton, and the game was *that* night.

I remember landing in Edmonton in fog so thick that you literally couldn't see the wing. The plane slammed down on the runway so hard that a bolt broke off in a panel above my head. When the Kings filed into their hotel lobby that morning, a little, elderly cleaning woman was shaking her fist at them saying, "You didn't treat my boys very well in Los Angeles." Mark Hardy looked at her and said, "Lady, it's 5:30 in the morning—go home and go to bed."

The deciding game was played April 13, 1982, and the Kings jumped to a 2-0 lead in the first period on goals by Simmer. Evans then got his fifth goal of the series, and the Kings led 3-2 at the end of the first period. In the second, the Kings got goals from Marcel Dionne, Nicholls, and Dan Bonar, and led 6-2 at the end of two. Bonar scored again in the third, and the Kings won 7-4 to eliminate the heavily favored Oilers.

I was so excited I wanted to call home, but the only pay phone I could find was located near the Oilers dressing room. The Oilers wives and girlfriends were in tears as I shouted to my wife over the phone, "Wasn't that a great game?"

TORONTO '75

The greatest regular season in Kings history was 1974-75, but it had a disappointing end in the playoffs. That season the Kings had the highest point total in team history, 105, lost only 17 games all season, and finished second to Montreal in the Norris Division.

The Norris Division was a strange makeup of Montreal, Pittsburgh, Washington, Detroit, and Los Angeles. It was as if the NHL made up the various divisions and said, "Whom did we leave out? Oh, yes ... L.A." The teams played each other six times—three home and three away—so the Kings logged a lot of road miles and yet had their best season. They went unbeaten in 16 of 17 games to start the season. On January 19, 1975, in Montreal, against a powerful Canadiens team, the Kings won 6-3 to move into first place ahead of Montreal at the All-Star break.

The playoffs that season featured a best-of-three series in the first round. This was a ridiculous setup by the NHL, because it allowed a poor team to have a couple of good games and eliminate a superior team, and that was exactly what happened. The Kings, with 105 points, met the Toronto Maple Leafs, who had only 78 points.

The first game was played in L.A. on April 8, 1975, and the Kings won in overtime 3-2 on Mike Murphy's goal at 8:53. The next game was in Toronto two nights later, and the Maple Leafs won in overtime on a goal by Blaine Stoughton at 10:19.

Due to a scheduling conflict at the Forum in L.A.—and the fact that Kings owner Jack Kent Cooke refused to play an afternoon game—the two teams played the deciding game the next night in L.A. This meant playing in Toronto one night followed by a cross-country flight to L.A. for the deciding game that next night. The two teams had decided to stay in Toronto and fly to L.A. the day of the game, but at the last minute, Maple Leafs owner Harold Ballard chartered a plane for his team, and they flew to Los Angeles right after the game Thursday night.

The Kings, who were an older team, stayed in Toronto and flew the day of the game, arriving in L.A. about 1:30 p.m. on game day. That night, Toronto jumped to a 2-0 lead at the end of two periods. Don Kozak scored for the Kings in the third, and the Kings kept hitting Toronto goalie Gord McRae with shot after shot, many of which he didn't see, but the Kings couldn't get the tying goal.

I'll never forget, with 10 seconds left, looking down from our broadcast location, seeing Toronto owner Harold Ballard and his sidekick King Clancy hugging and jumping up and down in the aisle as they eliminated the heavily favored Kings.

It was such a disappointment after a tremendous season that Kings coach Bob Pulford left the building in tears. Pulford always maintained that, because the Kings had older players, either they should have scheduled the deciding game with some rest in between or the Kings should have had a chartered flight home to get more rest. Because of Cooke's stubbornness, the Kings' best season ever was wasted.

BOSTON '76

In the 1975-76 season the Kings finished with 85 points, good for second place in the Norris Division. In the playoffs, they eliminated Atlanta in the first round in two straight games in the best-of-three series. Then they met the Boston Bruins in the quarterfinals. Boston had a great season that year finishing with 113 points, first in the Adams Division.

Boston was a heavy favorite and shut out the Kings 4-0 in Game 1. In Game 2, Butch Goring scored 27 seconds into overtime to give the Kings a 3-2 win and send the series to L.A. tied at one win apiece. The teams split in L.A. and headed back to Boston tied 2-2.

The Kings had an off day on Patriots Day in Boston, the day of the famous Boston Marathon. The finish line on Boylston Street was near the Kings' hotel, and we watched in person as the winner came in about 2 p.m. Four hours later, showered and dressed for dinner, a group of us approached the marathon finish line and noted that some runners were still coming in. My broadcast partner, Dan Avey, walked two blocks down the Marathon route and, dressed in a suit and tie, ran toward the finish line holding arms up in triumph. Some spectators actually started applauding. Did they think this guy ran 26 miles in a suit and tie without breaking a sweat?

The Kings lost Game 5 in a 7-1 rout, and on April 22, back in Los Angeles, the Kings faced elimination. As the Kings came on the ice that night, the crowd gave the team a prolonged standing ovation, dismissing the 7-1 embarrassment. The ovation lasted so long that referee Andy Van Hellemond told the Kings to start the national anthem or he was going to drop the puck for the start of the game. Unbeknownst to Van Hellemond, or anyone else at the time, the cord for the on-ice microphone ran near the visitors dressing room; and Boston's Wayne Cashman had deliberately cut the microphone cord with his skates. The singer *couldn't* start the anthem.

Boston had a 3-1 lead at the end of two periods. The Kings' Mike Corrigan scored in the third period, and the Kings trailed by one goal. Late the period, Corrigan skated in front of Bruins goalie Gerry Cheevers while chasing a loose puck. Cheevers tripped him, but no penalty was called. As Corrigan was sliding on his stomach toward the corner and away from Cheevers, he got his stick on the puck and in a sweeping motion sent it toward the Boston net. It deflected off Cheevers' stick, surprising him, and into the net for the tying goal with 2:12 remaining. The call of that goal was among the worst of my career, because I was so incensed that Cheevers had escaped a penalty call. I shouted, "Cheevers trips Corrigan. No penalty. I don't believe … Score! Corrigan scores."

I doubt if anyone listening on radio knew exactly what had happened except that the Kings had scored.

In overtime, I saw something I had never seen before—or since for that matter. Late in the overtime, the Kings' Bob Murdoch passed to Bob Nevin, who gave the puck to Butch Goring. As Goring came across the Bruins' blue line, he cut to his left and let go a shot from the top of the slot that beat Cheevers low just inside the left post. The Kings had won 4-3 at

18:28 into overtime, the longest game in Kings history to that point.

Then came an unforgettable sight. The Kings streamed off the bench, hoisting Goring to their shoulders to carry him off the ice. That's the only time I've ever seen that in hockey. On the radio broadcast, I was describing the scene and shouting, "We're going back to Boston. We're going to Boston for Game 7."

At the same time, down near the Bruins locker room, Kings publicity director Mike Hope was in a confrontation with Wayne Cashman, who Hope discovered had deliberately cut the microphone cord. He confronted him, and during the argument, Cashman swung his stick at Hope. Security personnel had to separate them.

Before Game 7 in Boston, Leigh Montville, an outstanding writer for the *Boston Globe*, wrote a story titled, "Kings of the Living Dead." The Kings had been shut out twice and humiliated 7-1 in the series, and yet, as Montville wrote, "They stick their fingers over the side of the coffin each time the lid is about to close. Two weeks ago, the Kings were a curiosity in Boston, now it's time to be afraid of the L.A. Kings. Man should always be afraid of things that won't die."

Unfortunately, the Kings did "die" that night, being shut out for the third time in the series, 3-0, to lose the series four games to three.

EDMONTON '89

The 1989 playoffs for the Kings featured Wayne Gretzky's first playoff in a Kings uniform; the best ever playoff series by a King; intravenous fluids; one of the greatest goals in Kings history; a rare comeback; a telegram from a former United States president; a Ukrainian priest; and a guy named "Lucky Butt."

The Kings took on Gretzky's teammates from the previous year, the Edmonton Oilers. Game 1 opened in Los Angeles on April 5 with the temperature 105 degrees. Kings goaltender Kelly Hrudey had been hospitalized with the flu the day before the game. He stayed in the locker room as the backup goalie. Center John Tonelli had the flu and was so sick he couldn't even attend the game. Kings goalie Glenn Healy had just recovered from the flu and lost 14 pounds during the game. He needed intravenous fluids between periods, and the Oilers won 4-3.

Game 2 was the next night, and it was still 105 degrees in L.A. Hrudey played in goal that night but went back to the hospital right after the game for more IVs and did not fly with the team to Edmonton. He flew up the next day. Kings forward Chris Kontos, who had played only seven games that season and scored only two goals, scored a hat trick to lead the Kings to a 5-2 victory. He had played earlier that season in Switzerland and joined the Kings late in the season.

The Oilers then won both games in Edmonton to take a 3-1 lead in the series. Only five teams in the 73-year history of the NHL had ever come back after that type of deficit.

Game 5 was played in L.A. and former president Ronald Reagan sent the Kings a good luck telegram. As they say, desperate times call for desperate measures. A Ukrainian priest from Alpine, California, in San Diego County said he could help, so he was allowed to speak to the team in the locker room before the game. He provided some inspirational comments, but his parting words were, "Just beat the shit out of the Oilers."

A guy named "Lucky Butt," connected with the *Mark & Brian* radio show on KLOS-FM sat with his bare butt on the Forum ice to jinx the Oilers. In 1988, he had sat with his naked behind on the pitcher's mound in Oakland; and the Dodgers beat the Athletics to win the World Series.

Kontos scored the first goal of the game for the third time in five games. It was his sixth goal of the series, and the Kings won

The Kings, en route to the Stanley Cup Finals, celebrate their Campbell Conference championship in 1993. *PHOTO BY ART FOXALL, COURTESY OF THE LOS ANGELES KINGS*

4-2 but still trailed in the series 3-2 as they headed back to Edmonton. Game 6 in Edmonton featured another appearance by "Lucky Butt," and one of the great goals in Kings history. With the Oilers leading 1-0, Kings forward Mike Allison had the puck and fought his way into the right-wing corner with Edmonton defenseman Randy Gregg trying to stop him. Allison continued behind the net, still with Gregg on his back; and then he came around to the left wing and put a shot between the pads of Oilers goalie Grant Fuhr to tie the score. That tremendous effort and goal gave the Kings the momentum they needed, and they scored three times in the final period to win 4-1 and even the series.

The seventh and deciding game was in Los Angeles on April 15, and again "Lucky Butt" sat on the ice. Gretzky scored on the first shot of the game, and Kontos scored his eighth goal of the series to set a club record. It was his sixth power play goal of the series, which was an NHL record. I remember more of Kontos' goals bounced off his body than off his stick. Gretky scored a shorthanded empty-net goal with 1:35 remaining to seal the comeback in a 6-3 win. After the final buzzer, Gretzky skated near the Oilers bench and pumped his arms in what appeared to be a mocking gesture, but he claimed that was not his intention, that he was just celebrating.

The Kings had nothing left for the next series, however, and even "Lucky Butt" couldn't pull them through. They lost four games to none to the Calgary Flames, who went on to win their first Stanley Cup.

CALGARY '90

The 1990 Stanley Cup Playoffs featured one of the greatest goals I've ever seen. The Kings were underdogs to the Calgary Flames, who had won the Stanley Cup the previous season. To stack the odds against the Kings, Wayne Gretzky wasn't with the team as they arrived in Calgary—he was back in Los Angeles suffering from a lower-back strain. It was the first playoff game he had missed in his career.

The Kings split the two games in Calgary, winning 5-3 and losing 8-5. When the series switched to L.A., Gretzky was back in the lineup, and the Kings won 2-1 in overtime on a shorthanded goal by Tony Granato. At that time, he was only the fourth player in NHL playoff history to score a shorthanded goal in overtime.

The next game in Los Angeles on April 10 featured a scoring explosion and another NHL record by the Kings. Three Kings players—Dave Taylor, Tony Granato, Tomas Sandstrom—all recorded hat tricks in a 12-4 Kings victory. At one point in the game, that trio had nine goals on nine shots. The three hat tricks in one playoff game set a NHL record.

With the Kings in position to win the series on April 14, two memorable plays occurred as the teams battled into overtime. With 2:23 left in the overtime period, it appeared as if the Flames had won the game. Doug Gilmour shot the puck, which glanced off Kings goalie Kelly Hrudey's pads and appeared to go over the line. The goal judge turned on the red light, and television replays indicated that the puck was in, but referee Denis Morel said he had lost sight of the puck and blown the play dead before the score.

The game continued into the second overtime, and at 3:14 the Kings won on an amazing goal by Mike Krushelnyski. Steve Duchesne shot from the right circle, Calgary goalie Mike Vernon made the save, but the rebound came right up the slot. Krushelnyski had been knocked down, but while lying on his back on the ice and a Calgary player on top of him; he somehow reached out to his left with one hand on his stick and flipped the puck in the air. Vernon, who was not a tall goaltender, was on his knees, and everything seemed to be in slow motion as he reached up, but the puck floated inches above his glove and into the net. Thus ended the longest game in Kings history—for the second year in a row, the Kings had eliminated the defending Stanley Cup champions. That was the end of the Kings' excitement, however, as they lost the next round to Edmonton in four straight games.

TORONTO '93

Kings fans had waited 26 years to embrace hockey the way they did in 1993. Actually, the 1992-93 season was a mediocre one for the Kings and held no promise of what was to unfold in the playoffs. Wayne Gretzky missed the first 39 games of the season with a herniated thoracic disk and didn't play a game until January 6, 1993. The Kings finished third in the Smythe Division and started each playoff series on the road. When the playoffs began the Kings won a high-scoring series against the Calgary Flames. With the series tied at two games apiece, the Kings scored nine goals in each of the next two games to win the series 4-2.

The next series opened in Vancouver against the Canucks and Game 5 featured the longest game in Kings history. Gary Shuchuk scored 6:31 into the second overtime to give the Kings a 4-3 win and a 3-2 lead in the series. Gerald Diduck had knocked Shuchuk woozy in the third period with a body check. Shuchuk went to the dressing room but returned later to score the game-winning goal. The Kings won the series 4-2 and moved past the second round for the first time in team history.

Then came the most memorable series I had ever been associated with—the Western Conference finals between the Kings and Toronto Maple Leafs. By this time, enthusiasm for Kings hockey was steadily building. Never before had I seen so many newspaper and television reporters on the road with the team. There were eight newspaper writers and five Los Angeles television stations in Toronto when the series opened on May 17.

In Toronto, we usually did our telecast from what they call "the broadcast gondola." It's located on the same level as the luxury suites. I arrived upstairs at about 6:15 and was shocked when Jim Fox met me and said, "I'm not working tonight." I asked why and he said, "Have you seen where they have us located?" I said I hadn't, and he said to follow him. We went up some stairs to a narrow catwalk above the main broadcast level and made our way to a makeshift booth some 100 feet above the ice. Jim is not too fond of heights, and the "booth" consisted of a counter and no walls. I walked to the counter, took it in both hands and tried to move it but it was solid. I mentioned that to Jim, but he said, "It may be solid now, but what about with 18,000 people jumping up and down in the building?"

Our Toronto television crew told Jim they would get him a safety belt and wrap it around one of the building's girders—that Detroit announcer Mickey Redmond had used one in the previous series. Jim agreed but said he wanted no mention of it on our telecast. After the first period, Jim realized our booth was not going to fall onto the ice, and he was fine the rest of the series.

Toronto won Game 1 but not before some fireworks. Toronto's Doug Gilmour had two goals and two assists, and with 2:34 left in the game, he was elbowed in the head by Kings defenseman Marty McSorley. Toronto captain Wendell Clark then fought with McSorley. Toronto coach Pat Burns was incensed and tried to get at the Kings bench after coach Barry Melrose. Burns told Melrose, who had shoulder-length hair, to get a haircut. Burns, who was quite heavy, was upset because Melrose puffed out his cheeks indicating Burns was fat. Later, when speaking of the confrontation, Melrose said he thought Burns was just ordering another hot dog. McSorley was so hated in Toronto that he said when he returned to his hotel after that game, his brother had cleaned up the messages on his voicemail. Marty said there were 102 messages, and 96 of them were threats.

The Kings won Game 2, 3-2, but the bad blood continued. With 2:43 left in the first period, McSorley hit Gilmour on the chin with a punch, but referee Don Koharski didn't see it. A few minutes later, McSorley and Gilmour got into a shoving match, and Gilmour head butted McSorley, but he got only a two-minute roughing penalty instead of the major penalty and game misconduct he should have received.

When the series moved to Los Angeles, the teams split, tying the series at two games apiece. The Leafs won Game 5 at home to take a 3-2 series lead and wanted to wrap up the series in Los Angeles, but Wayne Gretzky had other ideas. After the Maple Leafs' Game 5 win, Toronto newspaper writer Bob McKenzie wrote, "Gretzky is playing as if he's got a piano on his back."

There is a saying, "You don't tug on Superman's cape." After the pregame meal before Game 6, Gretzky told his agent, Michael Barnett, "The piano man still has a tune to play."

This is where the captains of both teams—Gretzky of the Kings and Wendell Clark of Toronto—rose to the occasion almost as if it were a Hollywood script. Clark, who had battled injuries throughout his career, scored the hat trick in Game 6, his third goal of the game coming with only 1:21 left in regulation to tie the score. Early in overtime, the Kings escaped a critical situation when Gilmour claimed he was high-sticked by Gretzky. The television replay did confirm that Gretzky's stick found Gilmour's chin and cut him, but neither the referee Kerry Fraser nor the linesmen saw the infraction. Even though Gilmour was bleeding, no penalty was called. Then, to add insult to injury, Gretzky scored 1:41 into the extra session to give the Kings the win and send the series back to Toronto for Game 7.

That final, deciding game, on May 29, was one of the greatest games I've ever had the pleasure of calling. There was so much tension knowing the Kings were one win away from going to the Stanley Cup Finals for the first time ever.

Gretzky said as he was going down in the hotel elevator to go to Game 7, he made small talk with a security guard about how crazy all the hype had been in the series. The guard told Gretzky that it wasn't very busy right at that time because the craziness would begin at 10:30 that night.

Gretzky was thinking, "Wow, this guys thinks Toronto is going to win, and it's going to be chaos here," so he told the guard, "Don't worry about your job tonight at 10:30."

"Why not?" The guard asked.

"Because my job starts at 7:30," answered Gretzky.

Late in the third period with the game tied 3-3, the Kings scored twice in 37 seconds to take the lead. Mike Donnelly scored with 3:51 left and Gretzky with 3:14 remaining for his third goal of the game. With about 2:15 left, the Kings' Dave Taylor had a good chance on the right wing but missed wide on a shot that would have given the Kings a 6-3 lead and put the game away.

With only 1:07 left, Dave Ellett scored for Toronto to bring them to within one goal. At this point, Kings coach Barry Melrose called a timeout, and he asked Pat Conacher, Dave Taylor, and Wayne Gretzky to go back on the ice when the break ended. Wayne said he turned to his coach and said, "I can't go. I've played the last three-and-a-half minutes of the last four-and-a-half minutes. I need a break." Gretzky later said, "That's the first and only time I've ever done that in my career."

The last minute of the game was truly hectic both on the ice and in the broadcast booth. I was sweating and became so nervous that several times I had to tell myself to settle down and just call the game—not to get involved like a fan, because I had a job to do. The final 50 seconds were spent in the Kings zone with the Leafs buzzing all around the Kings net with an extra attacker. I had the strangest feeling for about five seconds. A shiver came over my body, and I felt as if I wouldn't be able to speak. If I did say anything, it would be, "Don't let them score," which was hardly something you would want to hear from a professional announcer. With five seconds left, the puck was cleared to center ice; and on our telecast, I screamed, "THE KINGS ARE GOING TO THE STANLEY CUP FINALS. THE KINGS ARE FOUR WINS AWAY FROM THE STANLEY CUP." Several Kings fans told me later they recorded those words and used them on their phone answering machines.

Gretzky has said this about that Game 7: "It was such a big game against a team and a city—and basically a country. That's why I often say it was the best game I ever played in the NHL. Now, did I have better games? Probably. But in that situation, Game 7 on the road, that was the most fun I ever had."

In Los Angeles, fans were going crazy. I heard from people who said, on many streets in the South Bay area of L.A. and the Pacific Coast Highway, you could hear horns honking; and in the restaurants and bars fans were screaming and cheering. I remembered thinking that many years ago no one believed that L.A. would ever be turned on to hockey that way. I called my wife, Judy, at home, and she had invited a couple of friends, Dona and Randy, over to watch the game. I talked with Randy and asked, "What are you doing?" and he said, "I'm jumping up and down on your furniture."

The only disappointing part was, we weren't in L.A. to join in the celebration. We went right to Montreal the next day for the start of the finals.

1993 STANLEY CUP FINALS

The Kings were a euphoric bunch as they headed to the Stanley Cup Finals in 1993. It was almost as if they didn't grasp the seriousness of the situation. The Montreal Canadiens had won 23 Stanley Cups in their storied history, and a press conference was held separately for each team at a Montreal hotel the day before Game 1. The Canadiens were the favored team, but they seemed to be uptight and serious when their coaches and some players met the press. When they were finished, the Kings came into the room, and I'll never forget how loose they seemed. At the head table sat Owner Bruce McNall, Coach Barry Melrose, and players Luc Robitaille, Wayne Gretzky, and

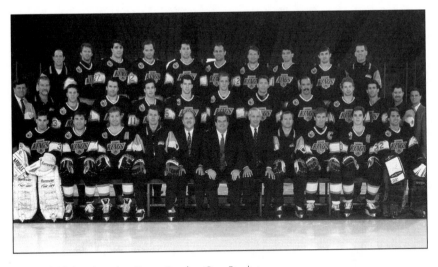

1993 Los Angeles Kings—Stanley Cup Finalists
PHOTO BY ANDREW BERNSTEIN, COURTESY OF THE LOS ANGELES KINGS

Marty McSorley, all laughing and joking. The Montreal press was looking at them as if to say, "Do these guys know this is the Stanley Cup Final, or do they think it's an All-Star game?"

Melrose had prepared his team this way. He told them in their first meeting at training camp that season, "If you're afraid to talk about winning the Stanley Cup, you'll never win it." So the Kings weren't afraid to talk about winning the cup or to have fun playing in the finals.

Shortly after we arrived in Montreal, I went to the press headquarters hotel to pick up my credentials. Coming back down to the lobby in the elevator a woman asked me, "What exactly is the Stanley Cup?" I was shocked—never in Montreal did I expect to be asked that question, and I started looking for Allan Funt because I was sure I was on *Candid Camera*. "Where are you from?" I asked, and she said, "I'm from the United Kingdom."

Luc Robitaille, the highest scoring left wing in NHL history, helped lead the Kings to the 1993 Stanley Cup Finals. *PHOTO COURTESY OF THE LOS ANGELES KINGS*

I explained to her that the Stanley Cup is the oldest trophy competed for by athletes in North America and that it was much like the World Cup in soccer, which I felt she would understand. Before the Finals begin in the cities competing, the Stanley Cup and all the other NHL trophies are put on display in a hotel for the public to view. As the elevator doors opened, there was the gleaming Stanley Cup on display, so she also had a visual answer to her question.

Game 1 of the finals was on June 1, and the Kings shocked everyone in Quebec by winning 4-1 on two goals by Robitaille and a goal and three assists by Gretzky.

Game 2 featured one of the biggest blunders in Stanley Cup history. The game was tied 1-1 at the end of the second period, and longtime Montreal broadcaster Dick Irvin said to me, "If the Kings win tonight, they'll sweep the series. The Canadiens will never recover." With 1:45 remaining in regulation and the Kings leading 2-1, the Montreal players were hanging their heads, looking like a defeated team. But then something—like nothing I have ever seen in sports—happened that turned the momentum in Montreal's favor.

At that moment, Montreal challenged the legality of the curve on the blade of Kings defenseman Marty McSorley's stick. I remember, when referee Kerry Fraser took McSorley's stick to the penalty box for a measurement, my partner Jim Fox shook his head. He knew the stick was illegal.

Coach Barry Melrose said, "I'll always remember when Luc [Robitaille] came back to the bench because he was over at the penalty box and I said, 'Was it over?' Luc started laughing and said, 'Oh, it ain't even close.'"

McSorley got a two-minute penalty for playing with an illegal stick. Montreal had a powerplay, and they pulled goaltender Patrick Roy in favor of an extra attacker and a six-on-four advantage. With 1:13 left, they tied the score on a goal by Eric Desjardins, his second of the game. When the puck went into the net, John LeClair of Montreal was standing in the crease in front of Kings goalie Kelly Hrudey. Kings defenseman Charlie Huddy pointed this out, noting that the goal should be disallowed because LeClair was not shoved into the crease. There was no video review of that type of infraction at that time, and referee Kerry Fraser let the goal stand.

The game went into overtime, and 51 seconds later Desjardins scored again—his third of the game—to give

Montreal a 3-2 win to even the series. It was the first time in NHL history that a defenseman had scored a hat trick in the Stanley Cup Finals.

McSorley's stick infraction didn't cause the Kings to lose the series because Montreal still had to win three more games, but it changed momentum so drastically that, from that point on, the Kings never had a lead in any game the rest of the series. All these years later, one wonders why McSorley was using an illegal stick—after all he only scored 15 goals that year and in his career scored just 108 in 961 career NHL games. McSorley accepted the blame saying that it was a "mistake" and that he "wasn't avoiding responsibility."

I remember how ecstatic Owner Bruce McNall was on the plane flight back to L.A. He was laughing and joking, and I thought, "Finally, this team is on solid footing and the future is bright." It was later revealed that he had to secure an emergency loan just to meet payroll. Nor did we know about legal problems that would put him in prison a few years later.

The first-ever Stanley Cup Final in Los Angeles was played on June 5, 1993. The Stanley Cup and other NHL trophies were on display at the Westin hotel and a steady stream of people, of all nationalities and colors, was arriving to view them and take pictures. The line started early in the morning and was still going late that night. Dick Irvin said, "I have never seen so many people lining up to see the Cup, not even in Montreal." It was another indication of how the Kings had captured the city.

Before the first game of the series in L.A., I did a live cut-in on our pregame show to comment on the atmosphere in the building. Just before we went on, I looked below our broadcast location and saw four season-ticket holders uncorking a bottle of champagne. They raised their glasses in a toast to something they probably thought they'd never see—a Stanley Cup Final in Los Angeles. I also remember the excitement and electricity in

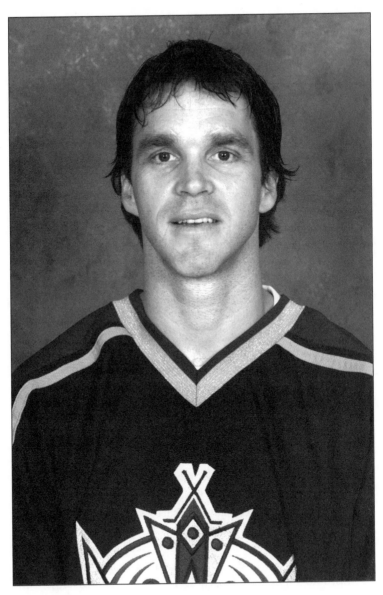

Luc Robitaille—Kings Left Wing, 1986-1994, 1997-2001, 2003-2006.
PHOTO COURTESY OF THE LOS ANGELES KINGS

the building as they paraded the Cup out to center ice prior to the player introductions.

The celebration quickly subsided however, as Montreal took a 3-0 lead in the second period. Momentum then took a turn when Kings defenseman Mark Hardy threw a vicious check at Montreal's Mike Keane and dislodged a pane of glass. The Kings then scored three unanswered goals by Robitaille, Granato, and Gretzky to tie the score.

In sudden-death overtime, during a goal-mouth scramble, Montreal's John LeClair had three straight shots and scored the game-winning goal on the third shot. It was Montreal's ninth-consecutive overtime win that playoff year and gave them a 2-1 series lead.

The next game in L.A. followed the same pattern. The Kings trailed 2-0 in the second period when Mike Donnelly and Marty McSorley scored to tie the game. Again, for the third straight time, the teams battled into overtime. The Kings had eight of the first nine shots in the extra period; and Jimmy Carson hit the goalpost. For the second straight time however, John LeClair won the game for Montreal as he banked a shot off Kings defenseman Darryl Sydor, who was sliding toward the net to help goalie Kelly Hrudey. Incredibly, it was the tenth consecutive overtime victory for Montreal—a NHL-playoff record—and they led the 3-1 heading back to Montreal.

The final game was played on June 9, and Montreal beat the Kings 4-1 to win their 24th Stanley Cup, one of which came in 1916 before the National Hockey League was founded. At the end of the game, Gretzky hinted to the press that he might retire, and Montreal coach Jacques Demers asked Gretzky for his stick as a souvenir. He should've asked for McSorley's, too. I've also heard that the gauge used to measure the illegal stick was autographed by Coach Demers and Referee Fraser; and currently belongs to a sports-memorabilia collector living on Long Island, New York.

As the Kings boarded their bus for a trip to the airport, unruly Montreal fans started rocking and pounding the bus, beating on the windows with their fists, and they tore off the driver's-side mirror. It was suggested that we all move to the center aisle in case any of the windows were broken. Later on Montreal's St. Catherine Street, some $2 million worth of damage was done due to vandalism and looting.

I was wondering what would have happened if the Kings had won. About losing in those finals to Montreal, Gretzky has said, "I'll say this until I die—it was the most disappointing year of my life that we didn't win. Yet, it was the most rewarding year I've ever had in my career because there were 22 players who believed in a coach and a system; who played hard, played together as a team, were unselfish. I had more fun maybe getting to the Stanley Cup Finals than I've ever had in hockey, and it's something I'll never forget."

That Finals series produced an all-time record for cable television ratings with a 22-percent share of the audience at one time. In fact, in the overtime of Game 4, more people in the Los Angeles area were tuned to Kings hockey than any other program on television at that time. Peak viewership in that game topped 725,000 homes and a 14.6 rating. There were more first-time hockey viewers than at any point in Kings history.

ST. LOUIS '98

The Kings have had some memorable moments in their playoff history, but one infamous moment came in 1998. It was the Kings' first playoff appearance in five years—since they had gone to the Stanley Cup Finals in 1993—and they were trailing the St. Louis Blues two games to none. In Game 3 of the series, at the Forum in Los Angeles, 187 seconds sealed the Kings fate.

That night the Kings had a 3-0 lead in front of a roaring, towel waving, sold-out crowd, and the Blues couldn't get anything past Kings goalie Jamie Storr. The Kings were just over 11 minutes from their first playoff win in five years when disaster struck. With 11:26 left in the game, Geoff Courtnall of the Blues slammed into Storr as the goalie played the puck to the right of the Kings net. Storr was knocked back into the crossbar. Kings defenseman Sean O'Donnell jumped Courtnall and pummeled him with punches. Courtnall said he was just trying to go around the net, and Storr stepped in front of him. Television replays showed a different story, however, as it appeared as if Courtnall leaned in toward Storr and made sure he had made contact.

Before Courtnall hit Storr, referee Don Koharski was calling a delayed penalty on the Kings' Ian Laperriere, so play should have been whistled dead as soon as Storr played the puck, but that didn't happen. When the penalties were sorted out, Laperriere got a minor penalty for boarding, and Courtnall got two minutes for charging so those penalties cancelled each other out. However, O'Donnell also received a five-minute major for fighting and a game misconduct. Thus, the Blues had a five-minute powerplay, and they did something few people had ever seen. They scored four goals in 187 seconds to take the lead 4-3.

At 9:59 of the period Pascal Rheaume scored the first Blues goal, followed 1:04 later with a goal by Brett Hull. Fifty-six seconds later Pierre Turgeon scored; and 1:07 after that, Terry Yake put the Blues ahead. The Kings and the sold-out crowd were stunned. The Blues had scored four times in 3:07.

The Kings felt referee Koharski had stolen the game from them. The Kings were upset that Courtnall got only two minutes for what looked like a deliberate attempt to injure Storr. Kings coach Larry Robinson was livid speaking of Koharski,

"He robbed us of the game, plain and simple. I can lose fair and square, but that wasn't fair."

Kings Captain Rob Blake had a different opinion, "It wasn't stolen at all. Mentally, the team broke down, and it cost us."

The Kings had lost their composure and focus, and defenseman Garry Galley said, "Once breakdowns started to come, we started to lose our poise. When a team gets rattled, it really doesn't matter how many veterans they have or how experienced a team is. Once the bleeding starts, you can't stop it."

The major question later was why didn't Coach Robinson call a timeout and settle his team down. After the game Robinson explained, "After their second goal, I was thinking of calling a timeout but [Brett] Hull had gone off the ice; and they didn't have their No.1 powerplay out there, so I figured if we call a timeout it would give them a rest."

The Blues wrapped up the series two nights later with a 2-1 victory.

STUNNER AT STAPLES

The 1982 Kings playoff series with Edmonton featured the "Miracle on Manchester." In 2001—in their new building, Staples Center—the Kings had a playoff series with Detroit, which featured the "Fantasy on Figueroa" or the "Stunner at Staples."

That season the Kings finished third in the Pacific Division with 92 points and met the Detroit Red Wings in the first round. The Red Wings were heavily favored since they had piled up 111 points in the regular season, second best in the NHL. The series opened at Detroit, where the Kings lost both games 5-3 and 4-0, and it looked as if it would be an easy series for the

The Kings moved to their new home, Staples Center in downtown Los Angeles, in October 1999. *PHOTO COURTESY OF THE LOS ANGELES KINGS*

Wings. As the series shifted to Los Angeles, the Kings won both games, 2-1 and 4-3.

The 4-3 win came in overtime on April 18, 2001. Detroit had jumped out to a 3-0 lead after two periods. Sometimes in a game, a team can be losing but creating enough scoring chances that you feel they may be able to rally and win. Such was not the case on this night. Well into the final period, Detroit was completely controlling the game.

With only 5:14 left in regulation, little-used forward Scott Thomas scored his first-ever playoff goal to get the Kings on the board. Thomas was only playing because Steve Kelly had taken ill with the flu before the game. Thomas had played only 24 games that season and scored just three goals.

With 3:22 left, Coach Andy Murray gambled and pulled goaltender Felix Potvin for an extra attacker. That left the Kings net wide open. With 2:27 left, Josef Stumpel scored a power-play goal, and the Kings trailed 3-2. Again, Potvin was pulled; and with 53 seconds left, Bryan Smolinski, skating to his right, fired from the right face-off circle and beat Detroit goalie Chris Osgood to tie the score.

The 18,478 fans, many of them wearing the red and white of Detroit, were on hand tying the all-time-record crowd ever to see hockey in California. Kings fans went wild— they had just witnessed the Kings score three goals in 5:14 to come from nowhere to send the game into overtime.

Another first occurred at 2:36 into overtime. Kings winger Adam Deadmarsh, on the right-wing boards near the corner, passed to Ian Laperriere at the right side of the Detroit net. He tipped it to his left to Eric Belanger, who had just jumped onto the ice, and Belanger ripped a shot under the crossbar for his first-ever playoff goal, the game-winner. Belanger was stunned for a moment, unsure if the puck had gone in or hit the crossbar. By this time his teammates were celebrating, as the Kings had snatched victory from what looked like a sure defeat.

The Kings then won the next game at Detroit to take a 3-2 lead in series and headed home to California to wrap it up on April 23.

The Kings trailed that night 2-1 entering the third period, but at 10:17, Deadmarsh tied the score and again the game went into overtime. At 4:48 of overtime, Deadmarsh scored on a rebound; the crowd went wild; and the Kings had won four straight over the mighty Red Wings to advance in the playoffs.

In the next round, the Kings met the Colorado Avalanche. With Colorado leading the series 3-1, the Kings won two straight 1-0 games behind outstanding shutout goaltending by Felix "The Cat" Potvin to force a seventh and deciding game in Denver. In that game, the Avalanche scored four goals in the third period to win 5-1, eliminating the Kings. They eventually went on to win the Stanley Cup.

AFTERWORD

HALL OF FAME

One morning in June 2000, I received a phone call from Chuck Kaiton, the president of the NHL Broadcasters Association. "Congratulations," he said, "you've been voted in to the Hockey Hall of Fame."

I couldn't believe it. Chuck told me I would receive the Foster Hewitt Memorial Award, which goes to radio-television broadcasters who have made outstanding contributions to the profession and to the game during their career in hockey broadcasting. Selected by the NHL Broadcasters Association, the honoree receives a plaque in the Hockey Hall of Fame in Toronto, Ontario, Canada.

The induction took place in Toronto on November 13, 2000, and my wife, Judy; our daughter, Kristin, and her husband, Gilbert; and our son, Kevin, were there with me. I was honored when numerous colleagues and friends from around the country attended as well.

Bob Miller with his family at the Hockey Hall of Fame induction ceremony, November 2000. From left: his son-in-law, Gilbert Gonzaga, his daughter, Kristin, Bob Miller, his wife, Judy, and his son, Kevin. *PHOTO PROVIDED BY BOB MILLER*

In my speech during the plaque presentation, I acknowledged those people who had a profound impact on my career: my mother, who worked two jobs after my father passed away so I would have the opportunity for a college education; my wife and children, who are hockey fans and gave me full support in my vocation even though I was away from home on many nights; and my on-air partners, the Kings owners, coaches, and players.

In that speech, I mentioned that I don't feel anyone—including players—ever start their career thinking of being in the Hall of Fame. Thus, when it happens, it is a tremendous feeling of accomplishment. I said I was most proud of my longevity with one team, the Los Angeles Kings. As of this writing, it's been 33 years. These days, when so few people desire to make a commitment—or in this business when so many people make a big splash for a while and then disappear—I am extremely proud that I have been with one team for such a long period of time.

That's what the Hall of Fame means to me. Longevity, recognition of a commitment, and lasting fame that will be visible for all to see now and forever more.

Bob Miller delivers his acceptance speech at the Hockey Hall of Fame induction in November 2000. *PHOTO PROVIDED BY BOB MILLER*

Celebrate the Heroes of Hockey and Los Angeles Sports
in These Other NEW and Recent Releases from Sports Publishing!

Tales from the Pittsburgh Penguins
by Joe Starkey
• 5.5 x 8.25 hardcover
• 192 pages
• photos throughout
• $19.95
• 2006 release!

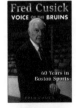

Fred Cusick: Voice of the Bruins
by Fred Cusick
• 6 x 9 softcover
• 200 pages
• photo insert
• $18.95
• 2006 release!

Game of My Life: New York Rangers
by John Kreiser
and John Halligan
• 6 x 9 hardcover
• 250 pages
• photos throughout
• $24.95
• 2006 release!

Striking Silver: The Untold Story of America's Forgotten Hockey Team
by Tom Caraccioli & Jerry Caraccioli
• 6 x 9 hardcover
• 256 pages
• eight-page photo insert
• $24.95
• 2006 release!

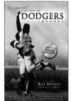

Rick Monday's Tales from the Dodgers Dugout
by Rick Monday with Ken Gurnick
• 5.5 x 8.25 hardcover
• 192 pages
• photos throughout
• $19.95
• 2006 release!

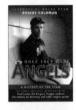

Once They Were Angels
by Richard Scott
• 6 x 9 hardcover
• 243 pages
• photos throughout
• $24.95
• 2006 release!

Fred Claire: My 30 Years in Dodger Blue
by Fred Claire
with Steve Springer
• 6 x 9 hardcover
• 200 pages
• photos throughout
• $24.95

Carl Erskine's Tales from the Dodger Dugout: Extra Innings
by Carl Erskine
• 5.5 x 8.25 hardcover
• 220 pages
• 40+ photos throughout
• $19.95

Tales from the Angels' Dugout
by Steve Bisheff
• 5.5 x 8.25 hardcover
• 250 pages
• photos throughout
• $19.95

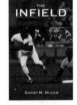

The Infield
by Barry M. Bloom
• 6 x 9 hardcover
• 256 pages
• 30 photos throughout
• $24.95
• Coming Spring 2007!

All books are available in bookstores everywhere!
Order 24-hours-a-day by calling toll-free **1-877-424-BOOK (2665).**
Also order online at **www.SportsPublishingLLC.com.**